Mile 0

Breaking the Multi-Generational Cycle of Domestic Violence

Pamela Miles

TABLE OF CONTENTS

AUTHOR'S NOTE

After I shared a small part of my story in an English class in college, my professor took me aside and strongly encouraged me to write my whole story, to write my truth and bring it to light for others. This brief memoir of a period in my life has breathed itself into being as a result of the encouragement from professors and friends along the way. It has taken almost ten years to finish because of procrastination and my own life journey.

This is my story, written from my own perspective. Some of the people I write about have been named and some have names that have been omitted or changed for their own privacy or protection. I know that others may see these events differently than I do. This is my truth; my story. It is always important to give voice to our own story and to speak our own truth. This is mine.

It is my deepest hope that through my story, others will gleam a glimmer of hope; a chance for a new life. I am a survivor. I hope more will become survivors because of my story and break the cycle of violence and abuse. I broke my family's multi-generational cycle. It only takes one to change the course. Not all those who grow up in abuse become abusers. Sometimes we become generations of victims instead, because that is all we know. I broke the cycle and I am a survivor.

PROLOGUE:

A MOMENT IN TIME

It was another one of those nights. I lay awake in bed, listening to the arguing, and the constant swearing. The dishes broke just as easily as the jagged words were thrown. This night wasn't much different from the hundreds of others I had listened to. It had become a weekly routine by the time I was sixteen. Sometimes it was more often; sometimes, there was peace for a month.

It always started the same way—"the children are putting a wedge between you and me," she would scream. And so my step-mother would curse and swear, accusing my father that his allegiance to his children was stronger than to his wife—which, in her opinion, was just plain wrong. He never really argued back, and rarely ever raised his voice in return to her. She would hit him and throw things at him, and yet he never dished it back. At least from my vantage point, lying frozen in my bed, waiting for the peace, so I could finally get some sleep before school the next day.

Usually the arguments would end with her taking it too far: she'd bring my father's dead mother into the argument, stating that he never had a real mother, due to her drinking away the cancer pain.

"What do you know about what a family is supposed to be like?! Your father committed suicide and your mother was a drunk because she couldn't deal with the pain."

When she spoke those words, Dad would respond in a quavering, almost inaudible voice.

"Damn you—you didn't have to go there. Damn you."

Soon I'd hear the front door open and slam. Then the car's engine would start up in the driveway, as my step-mother opened the front door to yell, "Go ahead—run away!"

Dad would peel out of the gravel driveway. The house would be silent, but the tension would still be there. For the next couple of hours, I would lie breathless and awake. Wide awake.

You would think after hundreds of arguments like this, the routine wouldn't get to me. I'd lie there, and he'd always return. But I never knew for sure. I had my doubts—constant doubts. The fear a young child has of being left stranded alone in a dark scary room was the suffocating emotion that weighed over me. There was that constant doubt that this time was the last time. This was it—he'd had enough. He'd never return. Not unless I prayed. It may sound like such a naive and childish thing to do, but I felt a security in those moments of conversing with the Lord. I would talk to God, asking—no, pleading—for my father to return to me.

"Please let him know and remember who he's left behind . . . me . . . with her . . . please don't let him forget I'm here. Please make him come back."

The idea of Dad being gone forever was too painful. I always felt that if I didn't plead, my father wouldn't get the messages, and he wouldn't return. Then I would hear the car drive back down the gravel driveway and the front door of the house would open slowly and quietly, hours later, and I knew he was home. Then I could breathe. I would let out a deep sigh—it had worked—my prayers are answered is what I thought. My step-mother was in bed, and he would join her quietly, and the house would be still again. Not a sound. Peace. Peace as I knew it at the time.

Tonight was a different night though. Usually after a few hours of arguing and the normal routine of dishes and furniture being broken, an array of words being flung, Dad would leave. The words were different tonight—they were harsher. There was a different "presence" in the air and I could feel this "thing" but couldn't describe it, but there was something different happening tonight in the house. I heard the mention of the set of rifles in their bedroom closet. My heart stopped. The next thing I heard was them running to the bedroom—a violent and frantic race. Through the massive bumping down the hallway, the loud, harsh words continued. Doors opened and slammed. I heard a struggle, I heard crying. I lay paralyzed, not knowing what to do—or even if I should or could do anything. I waited and listened.

This night was different; Dad didn't leave. He did something much different.

CHAPTER ONE

1979

A lot happened that year which ultimately changed the path of my life forever. The year I turned five felt like the prime time of life. There were no worries other than to make sure you didn't spill your Kool-Aid on your white shirt or accidentally snort a bug up your nose while running down the street. Who could ask for a better life with such childlike stresses? The second hand of life's clock seemed to have paused slightly during that year. There was a changing of the guard, not only in my world, but also throughout the world. Israel and Egypt signed a peace treaty; the British Empire freed Malta from their rule, as did Denmark free Greenland. Margaret Thatcher became the first female British Prime Minister; Joe Clark became the youngest prime minister in Canada; and Saddam Hussein became the new president of Iraq. It truly was an era of change, and only the future would tell if it was for good or for bad on all fronts.

My life prior to 1979 consisted of a humble upbringing at the logging camps where my father worked, and the neighboring trailer parks which allowed him to have close access to the camps without us living amongst their wildness. The wilderness of Northern British Columbia is where my life started, in a small place named Dawson Creek, population 700. The streets are fairly bare in this northern prairie land, and the provincial border of Alberta is just a few miles away. Dawson Creek is known as Mile

"0," as it is the start of the Alaskan Highway. What an opportune place to be born—Mile "0". Either this was meant to be a prediction of what my life would amount to—absolutely nothing—or that my life was meant to become the starting place of a very long highway through a wilderness land where only the strong survive.

Throughout my early years in life, my father was the person who governed our family. My father was a gangling thin man, with a brown balding tuft of wavy hair, which, even at twenty-seven years old, could never lie flat, and so he regularly hid this mangled mess under an old, worn trucker hat, usually displaying the green logo of John Deere or the bright orange Kubota tractor. His bushy side-burns were his attempt to make up for the thinning hair, and they matched his light brown eyes, where he proudly claimed to be a lookalike of Bert Reynolds. My father was always a quiet presence, not a man of many words. His frame, just a couple inches shy of six feet, was still the leader of our small family. He led us all over Northern BC in pursuit of regular employment, from logging camps to construction and truck driving, to finally being a first aide instructor at the local college at our last residence in Prince George. We followed in absolute love and belief in his steady guidance. Dad was gone a lot during those early years with employment wherever it led him, usually further away from home, where we stayed waiting.

Mom was the strongest woman I could have ever had during those years of Dad's absence in the northern wilderness. Her long, straight, brown hair and olive complexion were identical to my older sister's, where I was the stand alone blue-eyed, blonde-haired kid who stood out in a family of brunettes, not to mention the dark brown of the massive forests of the logging world. My older sister by two years was the usual older sister: a confidante, an enemy, and the first-born child jealous of now having to share her mother's attention. Although my young age of four seemed to condemn me to being left out of any friends until I officially entered Kindergarten, I was determined to not continue to be a bystander watching my older sister's friends and her play, leaving me stranded by myself.

The summer of 1979, the dark green and brown blur never faded and the heat never cooled at our home. The pine scent became stronger in these dry summers and the dust smudged my face, proof of a hard day's play. I dreaded the forest and its ominous size when I was four years old. I knew I could easily get lost, and I also knew better than to wander off too far. There were sightings of bears in our wooded trailer park outside the city of Prince George in Northern British Columbia. My parents said the bears lived in the wooded hillside cliff directly behind our trailer, and some were also spotted along the densely wooded trail to the school. There were times I swore I could see a massive swarm of bear's eyeballs staring down on me from that wooded cliff behind our trailer. These bears were the same bears I would overhear the loggers at the corner store talking about getting into the camps and going through the garbage. Even worse were the stories of the bears attacking the logging camps and the bears needing to be shot.

The trailer park was packed tight with single- and double-wide trailers. Most had a simple dirt drive that led under the colored waffled, plastic-fiberglass carport covers arraying the ground with shades of yellow and green. Although ours was a simple single with a clear covered carport that had aged and now was glowing yellow beneath, we were parked at the very edge and top of the hill, right below the "bear's eye" cliff. I always felt we had the best view of the trailer park—except the bear area. This landscape was barren except the metal tin roofs of the trailers and the fiberglass carports. All the trees had been logged out years earlier to build this parking lot for houses on wheels. Recently pavement had seeped in from the local highway, forming more permanent roads, which gave a sense of stability to our forest civilization. Trees grew along the outskirts, establishing the boundary to the wilderness or the main highway. We were a desert, bleached dry by the alpine sun, and I had the best view of it all at the top of my hill.

Walking to the school was a test of bravery. The trail was heavily wooded, and we had to walk through a large metal drainage tunnel under the highway to reach the school grounds. Kids commonly dared each other to walk it alone—it separated the babies from the older kids. Every time a pinecone dropped on the dry crunchy dead needled forest floor, one would jump, causing your heart to race even more than it currently was under this stressful passing, because the sound was imagined to be that of a bear following after you, echoing through the metal tunnel. Walking through the woods felt like being compressed into a funnel, with the large open playground field on the other side of the metal tunnel. I guess you could say, that was the reward for making it through the birth canal of the metal drainage tunnel—an open barren field, with the school building another couple football lengths still further to walk to. I hadn't yet made it through the tunnel myself, and was regularly taunted by my sister and her friends.

Angie, my sister's friend, lived a few trailers down from the neighborhood playground just around the corner and slightly down the hill from our trailer. She was the same age as my sister, but her mother smoked profusely. Her father wasn't home much either, much like the rest of the fathers here in the trailer park. She and my sister would spend hours riding bikes around the neighborhood, letting their long brown hair whip in the wind, while I sat alone in the small, dusty playground. There was an old rusty swing, and black rubber tires for climbing, but they got too hot during the summer to play with. My palms would sting from the hot metal chains of the swings that would occasionally pinch due to the links becoming jammed. The warm air that was forced to be present only when there was enough momentum in swinging, would give little relief from the heat. The large black tractor tires that were half submerged in the dry earth, only gave shade within their bowels, if you didn't mind the spiders and flies seeking the same retreat. My small hands traced the large waffle tread on the outside, and would pick at the cracking side walls, wondering what made them so strong that one could actually stand on them. I never went barefoot on these hot lava rocks protruding from the ground, their heat would burn my feet, but in flip flops the occasional side of my foot would scald at the briefest of brush against its surface. I would pretend that these massive rubber rocks of lava and the dry sands of the playground would be my island. At supper time, the little kids went home for supper, and that's when the big kids took over the playground, their loud voices and errant behavior bringing the police on several occasions. The trailer park felt to me like a desolate island of dryness; I sat in its center while everyone else rode their bikes around me. I didn't have a bike, but I had a plan.

One afternoon while sitting outside on the playground, Mom hollered for us to come and get some Kool-Aid she had just poured. Angie, my sister, and I raced to the top of the hill to the trailer, them on their bikes and me chasing behind on foot. As soon as my sister dropped her bike on the dry, crisp, brown grass in front of the trailer, I grabbed it as quickly as I could and hopped on. I had never been on a bike before; I had only observed riders while being circled in the playground. It began moving on its own, without control, until I realized that to reach the pedals I had to stand the entire time as the banana seat jabbed me in the center of my back and the cross bar caught my legs below. I was a little wobbly at first, but the breeze felt exhilarating. I didn't even realize how far I had gone until I was at the corner of the trailer park by the trail to the school. I grabbed tight onto the handlebars, took a gentle turn right, and started heading down the hill. By the time I got to the bottom, Angie and my sister were yelling at me to get off. I had no intention of giving this up. *If they wanted the bike, they were going to have to come and get me!*

Luckily in the haste of trying to catch me, Angie had forgotten to grab her own bike, so I had the advantage. As an unskilled rider, it was a miracle that I didn't crash when I rounded the corner ahead of them. The girls were fast on my tail.

"Give it back! Get off! It's mine! I'm telling mom!" my sister shouted, as her stringy long legs pounded after me.

"You are in so much trooooouuuuble!" screamed Angie, as she kept stride with my sister chasing after me, huffing so loud I could hear it.

I darted a quick glance over my shoulder, through my serious concentration, and yelled back, "Na, na, na na!"

It seemed like the whole neighborhood came out to watch the excitement. And so it began: the great chase of a little sister on her big sister's bike.

No matter how many kids tried to chase me or block my path, I darted and maneuvered faster than anyone had done before in the neighborhood. My legs pumped, my sweaty hands grasped the bars with ribbons dangly off the ends which whipped my bare arms, and the seat incessantly jabbed my back with every up and down cyclical round of leg thrusts on the peddles. But the wind was breath-taking. My hair pressed back and whipped into cyclones of blonde. I even closed my eyes a few times, more because the racing breeze was drying them out, but also to just feel like a bee whizzing through the trailer park, which no one would dare catch due to its madness. This feeling was the best in the world—magical and peaceful. Bugs catapulted against my face as I raced throughout the neighborhood for several minutes. It seemed like forever that I was loose and free, and enjoying this over-the-top adrenaline rush.

The growing mob continued in chase until I had reached the limit of safe speed to take a corner. I learned that with such amateur skills, one can only go so fast on a bike. It was there, while attempting to round the lower corner of the trailer park and begin my assent up the hill towards home, making a full circle of the park complete, that I met my demise. My small, lithe body flew over the handlebars and landed flat-faced on a neighbor's front lawn. When I rolled over and looked up, there stood my sister and Angie, panting over me. My body didn't hurt—I felt wonderful! The adrenaline still rushed through me, as I spit the grass out of my mouth.

"You're so stupid!" my sister yelled at me, furious at my escapades and lack for respect for her treasured bike.

Angie and my sister both glared at me as they turned on their heels, whispering and as they marched away, taking the uninjured bike with them as they left. After lying there for a few moments, staring at the clear blue sky, the crowd of neighbor kids departing, I finally dusted myself off and started walking home.

That last quarter mile up the hill towards home seemed much longer under that staring sun; probably because I knew my sister had already beaten me home and told Mom everything. Even at four I knew what "getting in trouble" meant. Mom was waiting at the top of the hill. Although she tried to show me she was upset with her arms folded, I'm pretty sure she was actually impressed with my courage and gall, although she didn't admit that to me in words. But I could see it in her forced straight lips, slightly smirking in the corners, and her sparkling eyes.

As I paused under her gaze, head hung waiting for punishment, she said, "go on, get inside you nut! You're lucky you didn't break anything!"

I never knew if she was referring to my sister's prized bicycle or to my own body. All I knew is I was no longer the little sister who followed her big sister around all the time. That day I had emerged as a rebel who demanded to be noticed and wanted to be herself: independent and fearless. Our traditional roles as big sister and little sister had been challenged, and I had won out as victor.

That summer as I turned five, my world also changed. Not just because of the infamous bike ride, but also because there were other dynamics changing in our family of which I had no comprehension at the time. World powers were changing in 1979 in countries around the world. And in our small trailer as well, a changing tide was slowly approaching our desert island trailer park.

I have great memories of the actual trailer itself, despite only living there from when I was two until shortly after I turned five. At the top of the hill, our 1960s single wide claimed its perch. The fake walnut-paneled walls with black seams made the hallway appear even smaller and darker than it actually was. Occasionally Mom would open the side door, housed toward the back of the hallway, to help get a breeze during those hot summers. She also installed a two inch steel pipe across the three foot wide hallway about four feet off the floor, so that my sister and I could play gymnastics. The six-inch spikes she drove into the wall to hold the bar and our weight went right through the trailer frame and poked outside for all to admire her handiwork.

I think Mom dreamed of one day watching both her daughters compete in gymnastics, and the bar was her way of opening that door of talent for us. Years later, being the shortest in PE gymnastics class, I couldn't reach my body between the unparalleled bars like the taller girls, but I could out beat any boy on the high rings, and I loved to twist and spin on those like a butterfly. They always reminded me of that bar in the trailer.

The kitchen was at the front end of the trailer; a full array of windows faced the street, providing a small windowsill where we placed plants. Mom had sewn the half-size curtains with the sunflower print, but they had faded in the summer sun. The kitchen was built with a slight curve to it, making it more spacious than its true twelve-foot wide dimension. We had exactly 720-square feet of living space. Storage space was limited in the kitchen, so Mom invested in quite a lot of stackable Tupperware. Standing on a small plastic stool drying Tupperware cups beside Mom, as the sun peeked through the sunflower curtains, my high point at the top of the trailer park, seemed even more righteous. Mom's long straight smooth dark brown hair with blunt bangs shined in the sunlight. Her olive complexion and brown eyes coordinated so well with the walnut walls and the light tan tweed upholstery on the chesterfield, she could have been a model if it wasn't for her short frame of barely five feet.

Those two rooms and the hallway are all that I retain from the inside of the trailer. Everything that was ever important in life took place in those rooms. The two back bedrooms—my shared room with my sister, and that of my parents and the small tight bathroom—were insignificant. The kitchen, where I helped Mom cook meals, and the living room, where we played games and did gymnastics, is where we lived life in our small trailer. That's where the memories were made.

Outside the front door was a set of hand-built wooden stairs and a porch. A small carport attached to it was built of 4x4 posts and corrugated fiberglass for the roof. In the summer it shaded the driveway yellow, and in the winter it drooped low with the weight of the snow. The sun shone blue and crisp through the thick frozen cold snow. Just beyond this carport was our side yard where we had a wooden picnic table. My sister and I would build an igloo in five-foot deep snow with the help of this structure. The winter snow was so massive in quantity, I even lost my pop gun pistol one winter. When the snow melted in the spring, the pistol was nowhere to be found. I blamed it on the bears.

Next door lived an older couple whose children had grown and moved away. Their single wide trailer was identical to ours, but it didn't have a covered carport attached to the side. We lovingly called them Uncle Bob and Aunt Alice, and we spent many hours with them when Dad was gone at the logging camps months on end, and later as he taught late night first aid courses at the local college. They had a television, quite the novelty, and my sister and I were allowed to watch soap operas in black and white all afternoon, sometimes to stay out of the heat and other times to distract us from grown-up conversations. Aunt Alice smoked cigarettes and Uncle Bob had a huge hard belly where I would sit and bounce. He was a happy police officer that had a shiny bald head. They were the closest to any type of extended family we had. Until that summer, I had never met any of my true relatives.

Mom used a great deal of energy trying to keep busy in such a deserted place. I sat with her and memorized flash cards on the tweed chesterfield, getting prepared for Kindergarten in the fall. Day after day, I ate her fabulous homemade Kool Aid popsicles from the plastic Tupperware containers, the ones that promised not to drip, but still did. I watched her make cabbage rolls and pierogis, which we would stock pile in the freezer. She spent hours making my baby thin blonde hair into pretty ringlets for my first day of Kindergarten, although later for picture day, those same ringlets were destroyed by my sister's special talent with scissors. Mom was furious about that, but she had a good laugh over it days later. Of course,

September of 1979 brought many changes besides accidental haircuts and adventures walking through the tunnel to school.

Dad's late hours teaching at the college had allowed Mom to build new friendships, some with his students who would come over for barbeques and canoe adventures on the weekends. My sister and I would sit in the sun-bleached grass on a blanket in the side yard of the trailer and watch the swirls from the coil-lit mosquito deflectors to keep the bugs at bay in the evenings. We listened to the adults laugh and talk until Mom sent us off to bed. Except for Uncle Bob and Aunt Alice, Mom hadn't had anyone else for company, so it was great to see her happy for these new acquaintances. Karen and Cheryl were students of Dad's who visited regularly, and they helped me with my flashcards throughout the summer.

Once, my sister and I even got to act as first aide class victims, while the students wiped away our red blood paint and covered us in bandages. That was when Dad's first aid students needed some practice on smaller children. This pretend world was so much fun. Looking back now, I am quite certain this perfect summer was actually far less magical than it seemed as a child, but for Karen, one of Dad's students, it was the summer when she began to work her "magic" on our small little family.

September was my Mom and Dad's eighth anniversary. Dad hadn't been around much in the years prior, except for the two times he broke his neck in the logging camps. So that particular summer was a great adventure filled with outings and many visitors, a welcomed change from our normally quiet existence. Lately Dad had been focused on the first aid course he was teaching at the college in Prince George, and he seemed different when he was home.

One evening, as Mom sent my sister and me down the hallway to bed, she hugged me last and just a bit longer, as my sister disappeared into our shared bedroom.

"Wake me up in the morning, okay sweetie? I'll be on the chesterfield," she said with a worried smile.

"Uhh, uhh," I mumbled sleepily, as I hugged her back again and skipped off to bed in my pink polyester nightgown.

I woke up early the next morning and noticed my sister was still sleeping. I tiptoed out of bed, opened our door, and stepped out into the hallway, remembering my special task to wake up Mom. The morning sun shone through the windows as I walked into the living room. The old worn plaid blanket was pulled over Mom's head and her back was facing me as I approached. I could see the rise and fall of her breathing as the blanket flowed with her shoulders. Eager to have some quiet time to snuggle with Mom, I placed my hands on the smooth soft plaid and gave a wakening nudge.

"Mommy, Mommy," I said.

There was a moan. The chesterfield wasn't the most comfortable place to spend the night.

"Mommy, Mommy," I whispered again, "it's time to wake up."

As her body rolled over, the body revealed a face that was not my mother's. My heart jumped in panic, just as it did in the woods with the surprise of a fallen pinecone. What happened to my mother's face? Who is this imposter?! Something in the dark recesses of my mind recognized this face, but I couldn't place it for a minute. Time stopped and I flashed back into my memory bank of faces in my mind. Then clarity struck. This was one of my father's students. This was Karen. What was Karen doing in Mom's spot on the chesterfield? My breath was stolen, and I stood frozen, trying to comprehend this shocking face that was not my mother's staring at me, as she began to sit up. *This isn't right*, my mind whirled loudly.

They say certain moments replay in our minds no matter our age because of the emotional attachment they hold. I can still see the dust particles floating in slow motion in the morning sunlight in that living room, and the snags in the tweed upholstery of the chesterfield. A moment in time. One that changed the rest of my life in ways I could never have understood when my childhood body reacted to the moment with such panic.

It wasn't until months later that Karen told me the graphic details that a five-year old child should never hear: My father had been staying in town at Karen's apartment during the summer of '79, in a rather hushed affair from college personnel and students. At some point Mom figured it all out, and Dad finally confessed. The night Mom asked me to wake her up, she attempted suicide because of a broken heart. She sat on the chesterfield with all the leftover pain pills from Dad's prior neck injuries and a large bottle of Jack Daniels. It was late when she finally called Karen's apartment, and she heard the mumbled ruffling of sheets as the phone was passed from Karen, who answered, to my father.

Mom cried her anger and disappointment and explained her farewell to him, telling him what she had already ingested. After Mom hung up, Dad called the neighbor, Uncle Bob the police officer. While my sister and I slept, Uncle Bob broke down the trailer door and awaited the arrival of the ambulance. In the morning when I woke, I never could have known the whirlwind of Karen's new position in our family dynamics, and how the changing of power was not one from my mother to her, but rather of my father to her.

And so my story of a long highway from Mile "0" began.

CHAPTER TWO

A NEW LIFE BEGINS

Within a month of mom's suicide attempt, Dad had us packed and driving across three provinces in his red 1976 Chevy van. It had an oval, tinted bubble window on the far back corner of the driver's side, and Dad had made a bed in the back of the van for us to sleep on during our travel. It was an era of no seatbelts and lots of freedom when driving. My sister and I slept surrounded by boxes and bags of our minimal possessions from the trailer. Everything happened so fast that I don't remember much of those couple days of travel. I know Dad was in a hurry, occupied and focused on getting to Saskatoon, Saskatchewan. We were told we were going to visit his brother Brian, and his Uncle Alex, and that mom was sick[1]. That's all we were told. I guess in my mind, I understood that to be,

---

1 Little did I know my father had done one of the fastest custody court petitions in British Columbia's provincial history, and gotten away with it due to clerical errors. At that time, custody battles were required to be approved only through the provincial courts; BC's being in Vancouver some 800km south of Prince George. I'd like to believe my father was innocent of fraud, and that it was whatever lawyer he inadvertently hired, but nonetheless, they petitioned the family court in Prince George for divorce *and* sole custody, which the family circuit court granted – even though they didn't have the power to do so. And with that simple flaw in the system, Dad was one of the first men to be granted temporary sole custody of his two minor female children. It wasn't until a few weeks later, when Mom was cleared from the psychiatric unit of the hospital that she found out what had taken place and that her children were already hundreds of miles and two provinces away. Thus began mom's pursuit of her children which would last the next four years, with us moving constantly

that Mommy would join us when she was all better, but she never did, and I never understood why until much later.

The weekend we arrived at St. Charles Place was filled with gifts and meeting family we never knew existed. "St. Charles Place" as the family called it, was the patriarch of the family's home, high up atop on the ritzy plateau overlooking the great Saskatchewan River. It was a house which showed its wealth, with crystal chandeliers hanging in the dining room, a full pool table in the finished basement, and a separate two car garage. This was after all a mansion compared to what I had known my entire five years of life living in trailer parks and logging camps. Great Uncle Alex, the patriarch of the family arranged for us to all live with him at 1912 St. Charles Place in Saskatoon, Saskatchewan. He showered us with attention and gifts. The combination of the smothering of gifts and living in a glorious sprawling mansion which was only a block from overlooking the mighty Saskatchewan River, was very exciting, overwhelming, and to say the least, distracting for a five-year-old. To say I felt lost and out of my element is an understatement. As a home welcoming gift, Uncle Alex gave me my very own red-banana-seat bicycle with large swooping handles and swirling ribbons off the end of them. There was a silver metal striker bell on the right handle bar and fenders over the wheels, with a rainbow woven basket hanging over the front tire from between the handlebars. My one and only time riding a bike before was on the open road in the trailer park just a few months before. I had never ridden on sidewalks, and this was a new adventure to ride within the defined parameters of the cement

---

in an effort for Dad to run from being served papers. The courts later realized their error in granting the custody, but by that time we had been taken out of the province and there wasn't much recall for them to brandish. It would lay solely on Mom pursuing Dad and attempting to fight and drag him back to court again and again to regain any visitation or glimpse of custody of her children. It had been a slick and cruel move on a hospitalized woman who had just had her heart broken after being confronted with the affair of her husband. I still struggle with who is at fault in this custody mishap. Was it planned or was it a simple misunderstanding? Either way, I was only five years old, and now on the run, not even knowing it.

drop-boundaries. But he must have heard wind of the tale of my bike thievery at the trailer park of my sister's bike and decided it was my turn to have my own. My sister, and I were in awe over the distracting magical change in our lives. These magnificent new lives seemed to come from another world. Outwardly we tried to show our acceptance to this drastic change and conversion, and tried hard to not speak of our past life in the trailer with Mom. But all the while, I wondered when Mom was going to not be "sick" anymore and would join us. I really wanted to share my new bike with her and laugh and play with her again so badly. But for now Great Uncle Alex was trying his best to keep us distracted and happy.

Great Uncle Alex—or as we simply called him: "Uncle Alex"—was a bachelor, and for the most part, had been such for all his life outside of the years he had been married to my widowed grandmother (his late brother's wife). It was a pact the three brothers had made when they left the orphanage as teenagers, that each would always look after the other's families if anything ever happened to the other. And so, the oldest brother, Great Uncle Ernie died in the bombing of WWII standing on a street corner in Brussels on leave in his 20's, never having married, and my grandfather committed suicide when my father was four, leaving his wife and three young boys to be cared for. So Great Uncle Alex married my grandmother and became my grandfather for a time, until she remarried a few short years later. He then stepped aside quietly, and had been a bachelor ever since. I think deep down though, he still loved my grandmother, because he didn't marry until after she died in 1979. That year held so much transition for all of us.

* * *

It was September of 1979 and the school year had already started. My sister and I had only been in school a few weeks in Prince George when our lives had unraveled. After things got settled in at St. Charles Place, Dad got my sister and I enrolled at St. Frances Catholic School. Dad had grown up attending Catholic school, and had always been a good Catholic (that's where he met Mom)—and so the pattern would continue on in us attending Catholic school. We walked the city streets four blocks south, and eight blocks east going through the caged walkway over the highway. I stood amazed as I walked overtop watching the large semitrailers and pickup trucks speed fast, hundreds of feet below me on the highway. The only thing allowing me to walk on air was this cement floor held up by a cage of mesh. It was truly amazing, scary and a thrill all at the same time. I had never walked more than the distance of the trailer park before, which was less than a square mile. The tall dry evergreen trees, falling pine cones, and silent scorching sun, had been replaced with miles of cement roads and sidewalks, loud constant rumbling of cars and trucks, thousands of sprawling city houses, masses of people, all which blended into a whirl which was intoxicating and overwhelming for my five-year-old sense of direction.

It was easy to walk straight to school at the trailer park, I only had to turn left out of our driveway at the top perch of the trailer park, and walk straight to the end of the road, where it turned into the trail which went through the metal tunnel, and the school yard was on the other side. But here in the city, and the noise, it was not as easy. Especially for a five-year-old going solo.

There was a program called "Block Parent" at the time in the city to help children in an emergency. People who cared about the safety of children would place the red and white sign in their front window which showed a child holding an adult's hand, with the bold words of "Block Parent" on it. Within the first week of trying to manage my way through the maze of the city blocks from school, I had need for one of these signs. One day while walking home by myself from Kindergarten (as my sister was all day in school for second grade), I got lost and had to find refuge in one of those stranger's homes. With all the houses and cement, everything looked the same to me, and I couldn't remember which way to turn after crossing over the noisy-pedestrian air-floating bridge. Thank goodness the corner I had stopped to cry on, did have a house with one of those Block Parent signs on it. The nice, older lady brought me inside and kept me distracted with her birds which talked and repeated after her. She fed me Chef Boyardee SpaghettiO's and kept me amused until the police came to take me back to "St. Charles Place."

It was interesting that we never referenced the house as "home"—no one did, not even Uncle Alex or Uncle Brian. It was always referred to as "St. Charles Place," or "the House." Now, maybe this had to do with the simple fact that it was located on St. Charles Street, but I wonder if there was more to it. Why had such detachment been such a practice in my family?

By Christmas break, I had mastered the path to and from school, and I also had mastered how to mix drinks for the three bachelors in the house. It was a common evening pastime for the three men of the house, (my dad, his brother Brian, and my great-uncle Alex) to spend the evenings watching Canadian hockey on the TV. They all thought it cute that the two little girls in the house could bring them things from the kitchen and they wouldn't miss a moment of the games.

My "talent" was being able to bring them their adult juice. Uncle Alex laughed every time I made them and I enjoyed his laughter, and so I was always eager to please and make as many of their favorite drinks as I could. He had taught me how to pour orange juice and a clear smelly liquid together, half and half. I would place them on a plate and balance them as I walked across the kitchen, through the dining room with the big glass chandelier, and into the living room where the bachelors lounged watching the game raucously. Usually on hockey nights I kept busy doing this delightful duty, not fully understanding what I was doing. But then I was five, what was I to know? It made them happy, which then made me happy. This is a pattern I carried for years, being a people pleaser.

It was during Christmas break that this waitressing ended abruptly. Karen, the woman Dad had an affair with—the college student—moved from Prince George and into St. Charles Place with us all. She was horrified by what the bachelors had taught us, and put an end to it quickly. Uncle

Alex didn't laugh as much after she moved in, and there was a feeling of walking on egg shells and trying to be perfect to keep everyone happy. I don't remember giggling as much anymore.

Three months into our stay at St. Charles Place, as Christmas approached, we received a parcel from Mom. When we had left in such a hurry, Dad had us leave Ginger, our orange tabby kitten, behind with Uncle Bob and Aunt Alice the neighbors. As we held this parcel….it moved! My sister and I quickly and feverishly untied the packaging. It was a puppy! I was so ecstatic! I knew we couldn't see mom because she was still "*sick*," but it was wonderful to have something that I could hold knowing she had given it to us. We hadn't spoken about Mom or the trailer or anything in the last three months, and it felt good to finally say "Mom" out loud. It was like this puppy was a part of Mom, and with every lick all the lost kisses and hugs were attempting to be made up for. I squeezed and held that little Beagle puppy tightly, not wanting to ever let go. Dad however, said we couldn't keep it in Uncle Alex's house and got quite upset. He said Mom knew we wouldn't be able to keep it. He said it made him look bad having to take away a gift. I cried for that dear innocent beagle to stay but to no avail; Mom's hugs and kisses were to be taken away again.

Later Mom sent homemade Christmas pajamas. They were red-and-white, warm, fuzzy, flannel, floor-length nighties with matching caps that had lace around the edges. My sister and I had a matching pair. I still have mine, along with the quilt she made for the harsh winter in Saskatoon, and my stuffed yellow fuzzy elephant with orange button eyes. Items Mom made; where her hands and my hands seemed to somehow stay connected when I held them.

After the incident with the puppy, Dad and Uncle Alex got the idea of taking everyone down to see Ernie, Dad's oldest brother, in Tuscan, Arizona for Christmas. Great Uncle Alex had a huge RV, and so the drive to the lower United States was planned and finalized. Looking back now, I realize this was just another distraction to avoid what Dad had done, and to stay running and hiding from Mom, as she obviously now knew our new address.

* * *

It was so odd and yet, at the same time, an amazing adventure to be away from the harsh Northern Canadian winter for Christmas, escaping to the hot, dry, sunny Arizona landscapes. The Christmas of 1979 was filled with a sense of adventure and numbness for my five-year-old brain. I was surrounded by the only family members who remained to me; my older sister by two years; my wifeless father and his mistress Karen, dad's two brothers, my uncle Ernie and his wife Natalie and their new baby Danielle, my Uncle Brian who lived with us at St. Charles Place and struggled with Multiple Sclerosis, Epilepsy and depression, and lastly the patriarch of this small clan, Great Uncle Alex.

The cactus-riddled desert of Tucson, where Uncle Ernie's sprawling house with a swimming pool existed, was an even larger mansion to my new familiarity of St. Charles Place which was still in severe contrast to the 60-by-12 mobile trailer cocoon I once had known. It was filled with a sense of fantasy and excitement and yet a deep swallowing numbness of loss because of its massiveness. Something was missing amongst all this amazement. Christmas time was different. Mommy was missing.

Our visit was filled with the monotonous adult chatter and visiting touristy places. There was a regular lack of attention paid to my sister and me as the adults got caught up in drinking and talking in the sun around the pool. There were the outings of distraction to the wildlife park to see animals I had only seen on Sesame Street, the old Tombstone boardwalk town with enacted gunslingers and dressed up towns folk, and the brief afternoon trip across the Mexican Border where Dad purchased a rather large and heavy emerald green limestone, hand-carved chess set that he carried back across on his shoulders, leaving me to walk the remainder of the time, as I had lost my perch to his new toy. My body went through all the required motions of a small child in these settings: the actions of excitement, amazement, and laughter, and yet there was a hollow emptiness continuing to grow inside which made me feel like I was outside my body watching this child who looked like me interact with my family. Something was missing. Mommy was missing.

I remember Dad taking time one afternoon to teach my sister how to swim, as we hadn't spent much time around large bodies of water until now, pool-side at uncle Ernie's house. The only pool time we had up until now, was the blue hard plastic foot splashing pool in the side yard at the trailer, or the public water fountain where we stripped down to our underwear at the Catholic hospital when grandma died. As Dad took my sister deeper into the pool, I sat on the stairs of the pool, up to my waist in cool water. The other adults were drinking and talking behind me on the pool chairs. Dad told me to stay on the stairs and not go any further into the water; that he'd come back for me.

Well, for any five-year-old waiting can be hard, and it seemed like an eternity. Before I knew it, I was walking into the water, deeper, and deeper, and deeper. But I was walking towards my Daddy, and was convinced I'd surprise him and make him happy. As I went under the water, with my eyes wide open, I saw his white feet move and float in the water in front and above me. The sunshine sparkled and beamed through the water, and the ripples made by his feet in their movements were so pretty. And then, everything went black and panicky. The next thing I knew I was yanked out of the water and tossed to the pool side where all the adults were frantic around me. Dad hugged and scolded me all at the same time with tears in his eyes, reminding me he had told me to stay still on the stairs.

"Why didn't you stay on the stairs like I told you to??!!"

He told the other adults he had turned his back to me, teaching my sister to swim, and when he turned around all of a sudden I wasn't there anymore; all he saw as he scanned the pool was my floating blond hair on the top of the water. That was the first day I almost died. To this day, I still can't put my face in water (even the shower) without feeling panic and suffocation. I've tried swim lessons multiple times, even as an adult. Someday I want to swim and not feel like I'm slowly going to die.

And so the Christmas visit at Uncle Ernie's had some excitement, but it didn't end there. I don't remember exactly if it was out of desperate longing for her smell that prompted my actions, or if it was truly an artistic accident, or perhaps it was my desire for answers. After all the excursions, attempts by the adults to distract, I found myself alone one afternoon, wandering through my uncle's massive house while the adults were busy elsewhere outside pool-side. This innocent childish adventure soon became a memorable picture still laughed at during family gatherings.

It was Christmas day and as everyone else was preoccupied, I found myself in my cream-colored cotton-pant pajamas sitting quietly, staring into the mirror of Aunt Natalie's vanity. Before me lay the palette of femininity: the large, brown painter's brushes, tinged with cream powder on their bristled ends; the child-sized soft cotton pads sleeping restfully on the top of a cloud of dust; the dozens of silver-encased tubes of reds and cranberries, which looked like oil pastel crayons, labeled L'Oreal and Maybelline; the endless scatter of small, clear plastic, flat boxes of square ink-stamping pads with miniature Q-tips laying nestled in the box next to them; and the fragrant tinted glass bottles with tassels and small fabric covered blow horns, much too small for my bike back at St. Charles Place. I would never class myself as an overly mischievous child, but before I knew what my hands were doing, the makeup found its way to my hands, and ultimately to my face.

Who knows how much time passed before someone noticed I was missing. But as the calls echoed throughout that large house, I finished up the last touches of my best piece of art. This was no sidewalk chalk scribble; this was a masterpiece of a lifetime! The look of the adults' bulging eyes upon entering the room were enough for me to know my family did not appreciate fine art when they saw it.

"Oh, my" were the solemn words sighed under my father's breath. "What have you done?"

My smile widened; I thought if I explained, he would grasp the beauty of what lay before him.

"I just wanted to make pretty," I said. "Do I look pretty like Mommy, Daddy?"

The adult giggles and murmurs in the doorway hushed as I mentioned my mother and they watched my father lower to one knee, and place his hands on both my arms which hung at my side.

"Yes, you do look.....pretty......pretty silly!"

His straight face burst into the laughter with the other intoxicated adults in the doorway. Betrayal flew me into a silent rage. I pulled my arms away from Daddy's grasp and folded them sternly as if I was the parent now ready to reprimand him. Someone called for a Polaroid to be taken, and my father lifted me airborne without any notice of takeoff. He quickly placed me on the lounge chair in the living room. The prompting to smile for the camera only infuriated me more. Despite my refusal to perform with a smile, the photo was still taken. A human Picasso had been placed before them and had not received the deserved rave reviews, but instead received laughter. I was so furious over their laughter. I was both hurt and disappointed. I sat there and sulked while they walked away and told me to go wash it all off.

Funny how decades later, I can laugh over that silly photo as I hold it in my hand now, and yet the pain and fury of that moment digs deeper into a father's denial to acknowledge his daughter's cry for explanation: Where was Mommy? When was Mommy going to come join us again?

CHAPTER THREE

ON THE RUN

Most everything has a different flavor once we get retrospection. Looking back on my earlier years has been no different. Years later, and after years of therapy, meditation and contemplating, and through the lens of an adult, I can begin to see patterns take root from these first five years of life. The saying "Everything I learned, I learned in Kindergarten," may not be entirely true; I think it's the first five years of life and everything it entails. It's not just kindergarten. It's how we witness the world around us from our minute placement in our environment. How we are nurtured, how physical touch and words are used towards us and around us, shapes our entire world and how we will interact with it for the years to come. These are the beginning keystrokes of our very programming; our molding and forming of our individual clay into the greater creation.

After the vacation to Uncle Ernie's mansion in Arizona, we returned to St. Charles Place. The co-habitation of the entire family in Canada; Great-Uncle Alex, Uncle Brian, my Dad, Karen, and my sister and I, lasted only a few more months. Grandma Margaretta, my father's mother, had died from cancer that fall, after we had moved from Prince George to Saskatoon. I remember standing at the end of her hospital bed as she died, and being too short to see her face, and only eye level to the folded blanket at the end of her bed. This is the blanket which forever signifies grandma for me: a pale yellow, loosely knit blanket that hung over the sides of the bed. I remember the long, large, black car which gathered us all into its bowels while it processed us down the streets, with the grey, cold skies above. I remember being told grandma died, and watching a special metal vase as it was placed in the cabinet in the dining room on a glass shelf, where the brightness of the large chandelier could sparkle upon it. I was told "that's grandma." I was very confused. How could a person go from being under a yellow blanket to being in a metal vase on a shelf? The simplicities of how a child's mind worked: People could be changed, even caged into an urn. People could just disappear and not be discussed anymore, and yet still be present on a shelf "always watching over us."

Grandma's death was just another layer to the complex and compounded grief of the family which was not to be discussed, just like mom not being around and not being discussed because she was "sick." After the extravagant vacation and distraction and adventure for Christmas at Uncle Ernie's, the realities of life could no longer be ignored. Uncle Brian had always struggled with depression, and it finally took its toll when we returned and the attempt to go back to "normal living" was being forced upon the household by Karen. Karen knew what was best for this grieving family, after all she did come from a healthy family not riddled with as many ghosts in the closet as our family. So we began living by her guidance and rules. But there is no amount of pretending and putting on a smile which takes away grief or depression. One can't and shouldn't ever be forced to be someone or feel something they are not. Being authentic is being whole, anything other is a lie which slowly kills oneself…literally. Ultimately, I think any attention off of Karen is what caused her to be unsettled and angry over the years. She was the newest member to the family, and she desired attention; not for everyone to be focused on dealing with grief.

I remember walking back from kindergarten at St. Frances, and as I approached the house, there was an eeriness to the quietness. Everything felt slower. The garage doors were closed with their dark wooden trim. It was a two car garage, which I don't ever remember spending much time in, except occasionally helping my father and Uncle Alex work on car engines or woodshop stuff. I knew cars were parked in there, but I was also told regularly how cars and garages were dangerous, "That's how Grandpa had died" I was told.

He had "accidentally" left the car running in the garage and had died of the smoke which comes out the back. "Don't ever be in the garage if the car is on."

Looking back now, I think that's why something scared me about the garage, and *especially* when the doors were closed. Death lived in there if they were closed. You see, most five-year-olds don't understand death or even suicide, and I was no different. But once again, this new understanding of the bigger world would be forced upon me.

As I walked into the house, the adults were sitting around the living room. Except Uncle Brian. Dad had me come sit beside him and Karen on the couch. I don't remember the exact words, other than "Uncle Brian killed himself in the garage today." Uncle Brian had an argument with Uncle Alex over the phone and expected Uncle Alex to come home for lunch. The problem was, Uncle Alex didn't come home like normal for lunch that day, something Uncle Brian had not calculated into his plans. After lighting the charcoal BBQ behind the closed garage doors, he sat and waited for Uncle Alex to find him on his lunch break....and ultimately save him from this suicide. But that's not how the day ended. Uncle Alex didn't come home until later, and Uncle Brian was never hugged again. This would now be the second funeral in a matter of months for me, and the addition to the growing list of grief and loss.

Uncle Brian and I were very close. He was a thin-framed man, not exceptional in his stature, but gentle in his presence. He was slightly balding like most of the men in that house, but retained a tuff of blond-ish-brown hair. His had the lightest color of hair between my father and Uncle Alex, whereas Uncle Ernie was completely bald and had lost all his hair by 21 years of age. Uncle Brian played the acoustic guitar and accordion amazingly well. He was a quiet artist, soft spoken, and rarely even shouted during the hockey games. He was a calm presence whom I enjoyed our neighborhood walks with. He'd even let me climb the occasional trees, lined along the streets of the city, knowing how much my inner little soul missed the trees which had surrounded me prior to the move to the prairielands of the Canadian breadbasket of Saskatchewan. These trees were much different though; maples verses tall magnificent evergreens, yet still climbable, and he knew I enjoyed a different view and perspective from up top.

The house was very quiet for a long time after Uncle Brian's death. He joined Grandma on the glass shelf in his own metal vase, always watching over us.

By Easter, Dad, Karen, my sister, and I moved out of St. Charles Place and into a blue two-story turn-of-the-century house, just a couple of blocks from the new elementary school my sister and I would attend. We had been kicked out of the Catholic school, and I never fully understood that as a child: "What did I do wrong? Am I not good enough? Why am I not wanted?" I learned years later, that the church found out about Dad and Karen having an affair (maybe it was Mom who told them in an attempt to break them up, I don't know), but until the marriage was annulled, we children were not allowed to attend. I learned at an early age that I was a disgrace to simply be. When the church did annul the marriage, Karen explained it to us as the church stating the marriage never really existed. So if it didn't exist, did it mean I didn't exist? By Easter, we were in the new house, on Avenue N, four houses in from the corner. My sister and I could easily walk to school, and it was a nice neighborhood during the day, but at night the street fights and stabbings weren't so great to listen to.

It was in this pretty light blue colored house where a new way of living began. It looked so cute and pretty from the outside; green lawn, white picket fence, white trim on the perfectly aligned windows balancing the Victorian style facing the maple tree-lined street. But it was far from pretty and cute inside. This is where I learned to live two lives. Where what happens on the inside should never be shown to the world, and the outside appearance must be of the utmost put-together presence. Behind those pretty windows nicely trimmed, and the beautiful pale blue which matched the skies, began to grow a new family.

I had a new mother figure now, and I was told to call her mom. I was told that my real mother was harmful and was trying to kidnap me, and to tell Karen, my new mother, or my father if I ever saw my Mom driving or walking by the house. I was never to get in her car, otherwise I'd never come home again. I began living in fear of the stories and images placed in my young mind about my real mom Ann. She was dangerous, unstable, a harm to herself and others. I was not allowed to see her. This conflict of what I felt and remembered about my mom Ann—who I now had to call "real mom"–did not fit with what Karen–who I now had to call "mom"— was saying about her. And so I began living in fear of the anger which boiled in Karen in our new family over the conversations of real mom, and the implanted fear of this mother whom I loved dearly and had known, now supposedly trying to hurt me.

Within the year, we moved again, still within walking distance of Westmount Elementary, into a little white house with black trim on the corner of Avenue L and 30th Street West, just across from the large city park. The park allowed for running freely in the grass, and sledding down the hill in the center of the park during the winter. We were also only blocks from the end of the large city airport, and could go and watch the large jet airplanes take off. It was another change, and another new adventure now walking across busier streets, but the streets were calmer at night here.

We had a large garden in the back yard which we turned into a mini ice rink in the winter, a hanging line for laundry, and trees to climb along the sidewalk too. There was an unfinished basement, where my sister eventually got her own room as we got older, and where the chest freezer resided, in which my sister locked me once. Upstairs were the kitchen, living room and dining room, the backdoor and the front door, which we never seemed to ever use—it had tinfoil covering it for some reason. Before my sister moved downstairs into the basement, we shared a room on the main floor, next to where the washer and dryer were, just off the kitchen. Directly up from where our bedroom door was and the laundry machines, was a bathroom, and then the skinny straight staircase up to the bright red bedroom with velvet black fleur de lis on the walls; this was my parent's bedroom above the garage. Red with rage.

Looking back, we seemed to be on the run. I didn't know it at the time, but my "real mom" had gotten out of the psychiatric ward in the hospital in Prince George, and had returned to the trailer to find us moved out and gone. She was then served with the divorce and custody papers stripping her of everything she lived for. She attempted suicide again. My father and his affair with Karen had betrayed her, but his stealing of her children had broken her.

When "Real Mom" finally regained herself in the spring, she moved to Saskatoon to hunt us down. Karen insisted she was an abusive woman due to her anger towards my father, and so arrangements were made to keep us safe, with no contact with "Real Mom" allowed.

My mom Ann, continued to pursue us and took Dad to court several times. The BC courts realized their error of granting custody in the wrong court and so provided Mom with free court representation to fight to win us back, whereas Dad had to finance his own lawyers to take on this battle. Dad lost the red van, and I think that's why we moved out of the blue house too, otherwise it was running from Mom getting to us, as she had been seen circling the neighborhood streets, and we were kept inside by Karen.

Eventually Dad claimed bankruptcy and Uncle Alex helped us financially. Karen began nursing school to become a registered nurse, and Dad worked with Uncle Alex in his construction business. Finally Real Mom won supervised visits, and I got to see and hug her again. I remember that day so clearly: the little Italian restaurant with bright floral printed booths and hanging bird cages and getting to have a Shirley Temple. We walked in the park along the river, running circles in the large gazebo, and everyone told us to not go so far ahead and out of ear shot, fearful of what Real Mom might be telling us. It was a tense filled visit, but I enjoyed every moment I got to sit and snuggle on my mother's lap, breathe deeply in her smell, feel her warmth, and receive her kisses. My mom, my Real Mom. She was back, and there would be no more running.

But a child never gets what they want, and as the first visit grew over the years to more visits, and even unsupervised visits once every few months, each visit brought with it pure hell upon the return home to Karen, my other mom. She didn't share well, and we bore the brunt of that anger in unfathomable ways for years.

CHAPTER FOUR

LIVING IN FEAR

I'm not a therapist or a psychologist, however, over the many years since my escape of the domestic violence cycle which poisoned my family, I have seen my fair share. I've listened to my therapists and heard their potential diagnosis of my stepmother and her behaviors. They have stated labels such as Munchausen by Proxy Syndrome (MBPS), to borderline personality disorder, even narcissistic manipulative abuser. I don't know if there is a proper label for the life which I lived other than one of childhood fear and abuse; an environment of pure domestic abuse.

The proper definition of abuse by the dictionary is to "treat (a person or an animal) with cruelty or violence, especially regularly or repeatedly." The definition of child abuse by the CDC (Centers for Disease Control) is, "Child abuse and neglect is any act or series of acts of commission or omission by a parent or other caregiver (e.g., clergy, coach, teacher) that results in harm, potential for harm, or threat of harm to a child. Words or overt actions that cause harm, potential harm, or threat of harm."

Karen's care for her new step-children and husband fit these definitions on all levels.

As much as I cherished the visits we had now been granted by the court with my Real Mom, I dreaded them at the same time. Every time I returned home to Karen after a visit with Real Mom, I was drilled on what was said. I began to naturally be on edge after every visit for fear of judgment, and then I'd be drilled further as to why I was on edge and fearful upon returning home as "something" must have happened to upset me during the visit. I learned early on that when I said nothing bad or upsetting had happened during the visit with Real Mom and I couldn't put into words why I was on edge, Karen didn't't believe that nothing bad had happened, and she would become angry and irritated assuming I was lying. What followed was a spanking, being sent to stand with my nose in the corner, or missing a meal. These were the minor punishments in the beginning. Karen placed these upon my six-year-old fragile, emotional self, until I "decided to tell the truth" about what caused my irregular behavior, when in fact it was her intimidation which was causing it.

So I learned the truth didn't matter anymore. Not being hit mattered. Being fed mattered. So I began to lie. I lied about my visits with Real Mom to Karen just to get out of being hurt. But ultimately I hurt the one I loved most, Real Mom. With every lie I told to appease Karen's satisfaction that she was a better mother than my own, her sick desire for retribution and judgment, she logged my false statements unknown to me, and it was reported to the court liaison. In the end, visits began to dwindle to a stop. It was my own fault. My sister did it too. We both did.

At the time our young view of the world couldn't understand the greater consequences of our lies. Saying simple lies of how Real Mom raised her voice, or got upset, threatened to steal us away, or held my arm too tight, all came back to hurt me deeper than the blows which Karen could have dished out upon my small petite childlike frame. I lost my Mom again because of what I said; because of my lies. Mom lost her children again because of our lies. I learned words do matter, and sometimes you can't take them back. I wasn't strong enough then to stand up and correct my lies. It's something I still struggle with today: forgiving myself for all the lies I spoke in an effort to protect myself from Karen's twisted wrath. How did my own mother forgive me, I wonder? If she could forgive me, then I must come to a place of self-acceptance, love and forgiveness too. One of the hardest things a victim of abuse has to face is forgiving themselves and realizing it was not their fault. Nothing was their fault, no matter how many times they were told it was. Understanding the slow breaking of one's spirit by an abuser is essential in realizing it will take just as long if not longer to rebuild that broken spirit back up.

There are certain moments burned into my memory from the years of abuse that reappear if I shut my eyes. The sounds, the smells, the strikes, the pain, the screams, the yelling. The most common was my sister and I being made to line up and stand before Karen to answer for our "walking on egg shells" around the house, and not listening, but freezing when Karen raised her voice in demands. We had become timid children after enough backhanded slaps across our faces for even glancing the wrong way, or daydreaming, or simply not answering fast enough or not answering the right way to her. Too often we ended up with a bloody fat lip, or a bruised head from being hit so hard we flew across the room and slammed into the wall falling into the crumpled remnants of a frame of a child upon the cold floor, or a heavily bruised cheek, to which she would state "look at what you made me do! If you hadn't moved or flinched it wouldn't be so bad."

The first thing I learned in therapy years later was how an abuser will commonly blame the abused victim: it is your fault they hit you, not theirs. And so this programming began to impede itself into my very bones and blood, and with every strike and every word spit upon me, I learned to believe I had caused this pain myself; I ultimately deserved it. I must be a horrible child.

I understand there were eras when children were commonly spanked, or punished by going to bed without the occasional meal, mouths washed out with a bar of soap, or forced to stand with their nose in the corner. But what Karen did went beyond this. It began small like this, but by the time I was in 3rd grade it had evolved into horrific acts to the point where my sister finally tried to escape by running away from home. She went missing for over a week and I became numb at that point. Officials looked carefully at our house, but protective systems commonly fail abused children when the abuser is such a good liar, and Karen was held in high regard by the medical profession as she was a registered nurse. She even started to claim that we children were abusing her. What a twisted turn. The woman who made my sister half bald by grabbing her by the hair and dragging her across the kitchen floor and ripping it out of her scalp; the woman who repeatedly told us that my father and her "didn't have to have keep us, and could have chosen to put us up for adoption during the divorce." The woman who caused so much psychological stress, which caused me to faint and ultimately begin to have seizures. This woman played her magic on the protective agency and there would be no protection for us.

A child can only handle so much emotional strain and overload before the body finally gives way. By fifth grade she had moved onto the belt for spankings, on the bare bottom, but it wasn't the belt strap, it was the buckle. I remember once I was hit so many times during her uncontrolled fit of rage, I had bruises, cuts and welts from the middle of my back to the middle of my thighs. It hurt to sit, to bend, to move. One of my close girlfriends noticed my struggle at school, and so I finally showed her, but I told her not to tell anyone. It was the first time I had ever shared with anyone a glimpse of the abuse at home. But nothing would be done about it; I demanded silence because I knew nothing good would come from others knowing. It hadn't when my sister had run away.

When my sister's fourth grade teacher sent home new clothes with her after sharing about the abuse at home, Karen became infuriated and defensive. Karen stated that my sister was purposefully looking for attention and we weren't in need nor was there anything wrong at home. It was then I knew Karen's wrath. She was so upset over this teacher taking pity on my sister that she took the belt buckle to her. We learned then we were always to put on a good appearance as we represented our family; our appearances and words ultimately represented Karen to the greater world.

Karen received praise or empathy from the world dependent on us, and that was more important than anything to her.

I think it is common as a woman to realize your identity changes drastically when becoming a mother. Your world revolves now around this small being which relies so much on you. Their very survival is dependent on you. But Karen twisted this to being about the attention was no longer on her, but her having to share the attention; that these children might supersede the world's focus from her to them. I believe this was Karen's greatest struggle: Deep down she had low self-esteem. I believe it caused both fear and anger in her which she took out on the most innocent which she could control and feel more powerful over. She lashed out without provocation sometimes simply because she felt insignificant or insecure. But she didn't just harm my sister and I, she hurt Dad too. But when does a man ever report abuse?

It would be common for Karen to throw dishes and items in their arguments. Some would hit Dad. Most times Dad would stand and take it, sometimes he'd walk away. One time she threw a cup of boiling hot cocoa on him in her fit of rage. And this is where the cycle of abuse and domestic violence is so hard to break. Dad grew up this way. He may have known it was wrong, but he was used to taking it, so he took it.

Dad's father committed suicide when he was very young, or so that's what is told in the family, despite the death certificate showing "accident". Dad's uncle Alex married grandma to take care of her, but then she later fell in love with a man named Amy. Dad shared limited stories of the details of the abuse Amy ravaged upon his grieving family and mother. Dad only shared that this man was a horrible person, and did horrible violent things to him and his brothers and his mother, and that he had a terrible temper. Dad shared that when his oldest brother Ernie was only 17 years old the family moved from a farm in Northern Alberta to Saskatoon. Amy told Uncle Ernie stay at the farm until he got the rest of the family moved, and then promised to come back to get him right away. Amy never went back to get Ernie. No one did. They just left him. All on his own. Uncle Ernie doesn't talk about his childhood either. So the cycle of abuse was existent a full generation before me and Karen's wrath. That's all Dad ultimately knew. He too, had been programmed at a young age to accept hurtful words and harmful hands. And so my life of abuse by Karen continued the cycle; the multi-generational cycle of domestic abuse.

CHAPTER FIVE

THE MOVE

1984 was one of my most favorite years. It was memorable in many ways. I was in the fourth grade, and stability seemed to have finally arrived. I had been in three different schools so far and four different houses. But I had now been able to make lifelong friends at Westmount Elementary in Saskatoon, and things were seemingly calm. December of 1983 Karen and Dad finally got married. It was a simple wedding at our home with only a handful of people attending. I was told that although they had been together since 1979, it was due to my mother and her relentless court proceedings that they delayed their wedding. As a ten-year-old, I really didn't understand what all that meant, other than the continued anger of Karen towards my Mom in the adult world.

Fourth grade was my first time having a male teacher; Mr. Martin. I adored that man! He was an older man with a British accent who had grey hair, but still looked like Santa Claus in his jolly attitude. He would share stories of surviving the Blitz in London as a young boy and how he had a gas mask hanging on his bedpost. I was introduced to Anne Frank. Fourth grade was when we learned about Ukrainian heritage too, which just fed my inner ancestral veins beyond what I could comprehend until much later in life when doing genealogical work. Fourth grade was an awakening in my tummy of butterflies whenever I got to walk to and from school with the neighbor boy Russell Smith. Fourth grade was also when Karen became pregnant and our family was to grow. Fourth grade seemed like such a wonderful year. I was optimistic. I was naïve.

June 6, 1984, changed all that. It was the day before my birthday and we were in the depths of moving outside of Saskatoon to a little town called Hanley, on a rental farm. Karen wanted her new child to be raised away from the city. So Dad, as always, obliged. When June term was to end at school, I was to say goodbye to all my dearly beloved and established friends. So while the move was in process, we still attended Westmount, being transported into the city by Dad on his way into work, and then afterschool we'd stay with my best friend, Liana Cook, until Dad got off work and could take us back to the farm.

The farm was a fabulous and fun place in spite of being separated from everything I had learned to know and love in Saskatoon. There were three "lakes" on the property, two of which would dry up during the summertime, the third dammed by a beaver kept its water, but all the fish would boil up dead in the intense prairie heat, leaving no fishing for my sister and me. The farm had a very long dirt driveway, and the only trees for acres around were those immediately boxing in the house from the wind elements of the dry prairies. Because we rented the house, the acreage was maintained by local farmers. There was wheat and corn all around. The nearest neighbor was a good mile away over the hill. The coyotes would holler and yelp outback of the house during the nights, our German-Shorthaired Pointer dogs would get into the porcupines, and the mice would make their nests in the old pump organ in the house. Otherwise, we didn't see many people. There was much quiet and isolation out at the farm. The water was on a well system, and it seemed that ours never dried up, leaving the local farmers to come and pump from it to fill their large water-container trucks on a weekly basis during the dry hot summer months.

One particular hot Saturday, Karen was heading into the city for work, and had asked my sister to make iced tea. She had never made it before so clear instructions were written down on the kitchen counter to be followed. The water was left with tea bags in it to steep and Karen drove off. The instructions were to remove the tea bags in 30 minutes and place the tea in the fridge. While we waited, my sister and I went outside to jump rope. Before we knew it, an hour had passed. My sister was frantic and so upset that she had ruined the ice tea, and was utterly paralyzed with what the punishment would be upon Karen's return. So, she decided to re-boil a pot of water and remake the tea, not knowing that an easier solution to over-steeped tea was to simply dilute it with more water. So a large pot of water was placed on the coil burner electric stovetop.

The pot was aluminum and had a lid with a plastic black knob on the top. The pot was set, and rather than watching a pot to boil, we returned to our fun and games outside again. As most 10- to 12-year-olds do, we lost track of time, again. The neighbor had stopped by to fill up his truck of water for the fields, and asked to come in for a glass of water, of which we were always happy to do service. As we entered the house, completely having forgotten about the boiling pot of water, there was a loud POP! There was smoke and a smell in the house of something hot and burning. The neighbor farmer quickly went to the stovetop and turned off the burner. He then went to pull the pot of boiling water off the burner. Much too all our surprise, there was no longer any water, nor a pot bottom! Upon pulling the pot off the burner by its outstretched handle, you could see all the way through the pot: the bottom of the aluminum pot had completely melted and burned off after the water had all evaporated out! He set it in the sink and told us how lucky we were it wasn't worse, and off he went to finish the filling of the water truck. We on the other hand were devastated. Not only would there be no ice tea for when Karen returned home, there would also be one less pot. Karen kept that pot for my sister's wedding gift some years later, where she mounted it on a plaque with the phrase "a sign of a good cook is a well-used pot."

That following week of school after the pot incident, a whole other type of tragedy occurred. June 6, Liana and I were walking home from school to her house, where later, Dad would pick me and my sister up to go back home to the farm. As we arrived at her house, Dad was already there. It was surreal and eerily quiet walking through the front door, where Liana's parents and my Dad were silently sitting in the front room waiting. There are very few times I can remember my father crying, but it was evident that he had been at that moment. He sat down with my sister and I and shared that Karen had miscarried the baby. My new baby sister was not coming home ever. Everything that had been anticipated for, what we had moved for, would not be fulfilled. And so the day before my birthday is always remembered as the day my sister Elizabeth died. She was two weeks shy of being able to be supported in a NICU at that time. If she had been born today, she would have lived.

It's an interesting thing about miscarriages. The parents, mainly the mother, are always supported in their loss. Back then, fathers weren't supported as much as they are now. But still, the ones that are left without any conclusion or processing of this loss, are the siblings who were waiting. It was our loss too. Our sister who never came home. And it was my birthday which was forever shadowed by the loss every year after.

Following the miscarriage, my parents thought it would be good to take a family vacation to the states again with Uncle Alex. So we all piled into the RV like we had done in 1979, and headed south. This time we went to visit Karen's family in Washington. It was on this trip, that they happened to look at the classifieds in the newspaper and determined that the wages paid more in Washington than they did in Saskatchewan. And with that, we were on the move again.

By the end of the summer, things were already in motion. Moving internationally was no easy task and took months to process and plan. I started 5th grade at Hanley Composite School. It was a large school with students ranging from kindergarten through 12th grade. The school bus would come and pick my sister and me up at the end of our long farmhouse dusty driveway. There was still too much whirlwind and turmoil over the miscarriage and now the move that I didn't have time to make friends. In two weeks we were sent to live with Grandma (Karen's mom) out in Strathnaver, BC. My sister and I, and the two dogs lived there for three months while my father and Karen moved everything to the states. I was allowed, as with all the moves we did, to pack only one apple box of my keepsakes. That was all. No more. It was always hard to get rid of stuff. I had been given farewell cards from all my classmates in Mr. Martin's class, and I dearly wanted to keep them, but there was no room. There was always limited room for memories and keepsakes it felt. We were to "move on." So I chose wisely what was dearest to me. Always keeping anything Real Mom had made or given me over friends and other knickknacks.

Living at grandma's farm in northern British Colombia was an adventure and a much needed distraction from the loss of my sister Elizabeth and another move. Grandma was the only grandma I had really ever known. This was Karen's mother, but accepted and welcomed us step-children as her own grandchildren. Grandma was a tough woman, knowing and capable around any and all aspects of farming. There were chickens to feed and eggs to collect every morning, goats and cows to be milked, dogs to be fed, and horses to be let out into the pasture. This was deep back woods country, and we weren't to go wandering around out by ourselves like we did on the Hanley Farm to the lakes and such. Here, there were bears, coyotes, wolves, moose, deer, and mountain lions. Animals you didn't want to spook or get in between their food or offspring.

Grandma was a lean and well-built woman. She was strong, with not an ounce of fat on her. She had a short pixie cut and fondly wore a worn tattered straw hat on her head. She didn't care if her hair was peppered grey, and the lines on her face told you easily when she was serious and when she was happy. She attempted to teach "ladies manners" but could curse on a dime too. Grandma was also hugely into the company Amway at the time. And with that, we were forced to have these horse sized pills of healthy alfalfa every morning with breakfast. Breakfast was simple but she made it fun: porridge and hot cocoa. However the porridge would be dyed the colour of her choosing for the day. It always made it a bit more fun. Sometimes it would be red, or green; you never knew what the day would serve up! But the attempt of my small throat to swallow down those darn alfalfa vitamins every morning, made my hot cocoa always taste like the horse stalls. To this day, I can't drink hot cocoa without tasting alfalfa.

There was no city extravagances at Grandma's farm. Limited running water and electricity. We had a hand pump for water outside the front porch, and a woodstove for cooking and keeping the house warm. We had an outhouse, and baths consisted of about two inches of water boiled on the woodstove while the cold water came from the tap. We had bedpans under our beds for any night time needs. It was certainly a different way of living. It was hard, but it was very freeing in many ways. My sister and I walked to the Strathnaver school house which was two miles down a dirt road. When the snow came, we would walk part way, then sled down Dyes Hill on an old red wooden runner-sled, and walk the remaining way.

Coming home from school, was definitely uphill for two miles. Mrs. Hatfield (yes, one of the relatives of the actual Hatfields and McCoys feud of the south) lived in a wooden house along the road which we walked to school. Sometimes she would call us in to give us a warm cup of Russian Tea on our way home. Oh, how magnificent that was on a cold snowy day walking home. Her house was filled with an abundance of trinkets and knickknacks, and always had a warm orange-like glow on the inside to it. Both she and her house were always so warm and welcoming, and the tea was fabulous too!

Halloween was a difficult day that year, not just because we were in transition but because I woke in the middle of the night to a gunshot. We learned the next day that the two dogs we had brought with us, Spice and Blitzen (German shorthaired pointers), had died in the night. I was later told that they were actually put down, because of some cancerous growths. This is how things were done on the farm. No veterinary fuss or expense.

I cried for several days, as I had loved those dogs immensely. During all the moves in Saskatoon, these dogs, which came with Karen, had brought great joy to me. When Karen was angry and abusive, I could always snuggle with the dogs for comfort. Blitzen was my favorite. He was a deep chocolate brown and very muscular. Spice was a dainty little speckled dog and she was definitely Karen's favorite. Blitzen had been Grandpa's (Karen's dad) dog, but after his and Grandma's divorce, we took Blitzen in. Blitzen and I became best of friends. The dogs were really the last tie to Canada before the move to the States, and now they were gone.

I didn't know when or if I'd ever see Real Mom again, as I was told she wasn't allowed to cross the border. And so, I spent the fall months of 1984 being educated on the roughness of the northern frontier, while also being distracted from the impending new life another country would bring. I never longed for Dad or Karen during this time away. Grandma kept us busy enough. I know that it hurt Karen's feelings to hear we were thriving just fine without her.

A week before Christmas 1984, Dad and Karen arrived at the farm to pack us up and drive us south to Washington State. I loved Grandma's farm. I loved its relaxed, low-stress feel. Its freedom. I loved its quiet. Grandma never raised her voice or yelled at us. She never hit us. I also loved the two room school house which had 5th-7th grades in one class and the lower grades in another. There were only two other 5th graders, and I finally had close friends again. I loved the French teacher and the Russian Tea stops at Mrs. Hatfield's house. I loved the quiet of the woods, falling leaves and snow, chirping birds and the reliable routine of the farm chores. I loved the simplicity of the wood stove and its crackling, and the gorgeous beauty of the white birch leaves billowing in the autumn breezes. I loved the depth and quietness of the feet and feet of snow. The farm felt like home and it felt safe. And maybe that's the most important thing; it felt safe. For all its wildness, it felt the safest I had felt in a long time.

CHAPTER SIX

THE STATES

As we drove further south and away from Grandma's farm, the snow disappeared and greener lands appeared. The border agents finger-printed us and took our pictures at the border crossing at midnight and gave us our papers. Everything was in order. But was it?

I went from prairies to northern lands to a rainforest. The shock was overwhelming. The claustrophobia was suffocating. Where once I could see for miles, I couldn't see past the large quantities of soaking wet moss hanging off of every limb on the trees as they sprawled into such denseness, one could not see deeply forward at all. There was no telling what was coming or what was in front of me through these thick woods. Much like the life I was about to begin in the States.

Our first house was in Duvall, Washington off of Big Rock Road. A nice little blue house set back from the road, up a dirt driveway on a hill, surrounded by thick overgrown mossy covered vine maples. The main road was lined with trees, including some rather large cherry trees which mingled in with the power lines, something I learned while climbing up to pick cherries later. There was a separate shed across the drive at the top by the house, which Dad used as his shop to work on cars. There was a back overgrown acre of tall grass with a handful of large cottonwood trees and a pile of old wood beams with their rusty nails still in them. I have a scar from that pile of wood and nails, from when my sister and I were told to restack the wood, and as we fought over a piece, each holding firmly to the opposite ends, she purposely let go of her end, making me fall back into the pile of wood and the spiky nails. A rusty nail went right into my left calf three inches deep. It was also in this back yard where I would have my one and only "run-away from home" episode, where I climbed the big cottonwood tree, intending to never come down and return to the house. Dad came out after it had been dark for a few hours and instructed me to come down.

"No!" I said.

"Then I'll come up and get you and bring you down!" he said in the dark below. I didn't want him to fall and hurt himself, and so I came down. The furthest I ran away from home was my back yard.

We had enough privacy that we never saw neighbors from the house. The house itself had two levels. The main door off the side entered directly into the kitchen, followed by the dining room. As you turned left from the dining room, you entered into the living room where there was a wood stove and the pump organ. There were large windows looking out into the front yard facing the cherry trees, front road and driveway which allowed lots of sunshine to come in, when there actually was sunshine in Washington. Off of the living room, on either side of the wood stove were two doors to two bedrooms. One would come to belong to my newly born brother, and the other to my parents. Between the dining room and living room was a small dark recess in the wall, which was the entrance to the steep stairwell. At the top of the turn in the stairwell to the right was another bedroom with a door, which became my grandfather's for a time during his stay with us. He was such a deep sleeper he needed three alarm clocks to wake up! To the right of the top of the stairwell, continued the slanted roofline and shortened walls of an upper attic-turned-finished upper room, which provided the shared room for my sister and me.

When we arrived at our new home my sister and I were informed that a new baby was on the way. With Karen's prior miscarriage, all precautions were taken and she was put on strict bedrest for most of her pregnancy. This made most of the chores and care of our new home put on my sister and me. Grandma had prepared us well though. But as anyone can imagine, bed bound can cause agitation and short tempers. Karen already had a short temper, so it only became worse.

I attended Cherry Valley Elementary while my sister attended another school for older students in Carnation, and for the first time, we were separated in school. I didn't follow in her shadow anymore. I made some wonderful friends, one in particular named Stephanie. Many of the other girls looked at my second hand clothes and would tease, and ask me what "label" it was. I didn't know what a label was, which just caused me more humiliation and more bullying. But Stephanie was small like me and knew how to hold her own against the big bullies. She was petite with beautiful skin and some small freckles and gorgeous brown long curly hair, which she always wore pulled back into a braid; it was beautiful hair. I was never allowed long hair like I wanted, and Karen always cut my hair short like a boy, something I truly was embarrassed about and hated. Because of Stephanie's popularity and friendliness, she had me making friends with many of the girls in her circle in no time. Summer brought sleep overs at Stephanie's and getting out of the house away from Karen.

Summer also brought my new baby brother. He was born a month early, but this time the baby was going to live. James was a bundle of joy, but it also brought more harshness from Karen. This was her child, and then there was my sister and me. She always said she treated my sister and I as if we were her own, but I know that wasn't true. There was a difference, a big difference. Dad was gone at work a lot between commuting all the way to Issaquah and back to Duvall, plus his eight hours in the office, and so he always missed the treatment she dished out after school.

One fall afternoon, she was yelling at me for something I had done. She lectured me as we stood a few feet away from the woodstove by the antique pump organ. She was skilled at lecturing and yelling, which could last over an hour at times. I was getting overheated, but she continued her rampage, even when I asked to sit down. Next thing I know, I woke up on the floor. I had barely missed falling onto the woodstove like one of my great-aunts had back in the day. When I awoke, I knew this feeling. It had happened before. I was sure I had fainted and was going to be in even more trouble, as had happened so many times in Canada. But this time was different. Karen looked panicked. Dad was called home from work and I was raced to the nearby hospital and had an EEG done and was diagnosed with epilepsy. I was placed on anti-seizure drugs. My "seizure" had lasted about 30 seconds, she told the doctor, and I had twitched while unconscious. I remember when I fainted while being yelled at as a child in Canada that I was "fake-fainting."

"You don't move when you faint," she'd scream and make me stand back up while my knees were still weak. I didn't understand the difference this one was from the others. But nonetheless, I got the label as an epileptic.

It seemed like Karen thrived off having a child with a diagnosis. Everyone at school needed to be told and educated on how to handle me if I had a seizure. I wasn't allowed to have deep baths anymore. I wasn't allowed to be alone with the baby. Everything changed. I was somehow "less than" or "abnormal" and yet she flipped a switch and loved the attention all the doctors gave her for diagnosing and catching this in her child. She got to interface at a more personal level with all her medical peers, and she loved the attention it brought her. But it didn't stop the abuse.

One day she didn't just take the belt to me to release her rage, she turned and used the buckle instead on my bare bottom. I was left with cuts, bruises and welts for weeks. I showed my friend Stephanie, and asked her to never tell. It was the only time I ever shared what really went on behind closed doors in my home. I remembered what happened to my sister when she shared in Canada, and I didn't want the same punishments to come down on me. So Stephanie never told anyone to my knowledge. I wonder what would have happened if she had. Would anyone have believed me, with the marks on my backside, from the middle of my back to the back of my knees? Would Karen have convinced the authorities again that she was a medical professional as a registered nurse, and it was the children abusing her, as she did before with my sister?

I only got a year with my friends at Cherry Valley before we moved yet again. I had a wonderful teacher that year though, Mr. Beeman, who seemed to understand me. He was at least six feet tall, double my height it felt, and would bend down on one knee to speak to me in the most caring voice.

"Good morning, Miss Pam," he'd welcome me every day, bent down on his one knee. He was still taller than me when he knelt down!

Here was an adult who actually looked me in the eye and listened to me. I felt like I could trust him with anything. He looked out for me with my new diagnosis, and he made it like it was no big deal and treated me normally. He made the point that I had no limits in his class. I even won the class spelling bee and made it to the all-school spelling bee. Mr. Beeman was always so encouraging. I was so sad to move again, especially from a dear friend who knew my truth, something Liana never knew, and a teacher who truly saw me and cared for me.

This time we moved to the neighboring town of Woodinville. It was 1986 and the middle of 6th grade, and once again I didn't fit in at the new school with my haircut and second hand clothes. I didn't have a Stephanie there to help me along or a Mr. Beeman either. The bullies here were much worse.

It started out with small things like name calling. Then one day after recess, I came back to my desk to find my personalized ruler inscribed with an "S" at the front of my name to spell "SPAM." Later at another recess, as I wore a tan second-hand trench coat (another item the bullies loved to tease me over), I was called over to the far back fence of the playground. There I was tied backwards to the chain-link fence by the trench coat waist-ties behind my back, and was left out there when the recess bell rang. The worst, which I still carry the scars from, happened one day on the school bus. I had my hands on the top of the seat in front of me. A boy who didn't like me sat up tall in the seat whose backing I had my hand on, turned around and told me to get my hands off of his seat. I said no. He ferociously began to attack my hands with his nails, ripping the back of my hands up severely in a matter of seconds. It was like he had cat claws. I went to the nurse's office upon arriving at school, and she bandaged me up, and the student got into trouble. I still have those marks of his claws on the backs of my hands. So it is simple to say, Wellington Elementary and the 6th grade were not good to me.

Between being bullied and beaten at home and bullied and teased at school, I began dreading everything. My self-esteem was none existent. For the first time I felt utterly hopeless. And I had no-one to turn to. I felt so alone. My sister seemed to be in more trouble than I was, and so she seemed to take the brunt of most of Karen's anger in those days. I learned to stay as low as I could on the radar in hopes of not getting knocked across the room with Karen's hand and being the recipient of a bloodied lip. Dad seemed too busy at work, and when he'd come home, Karen would complain about how bad we'd been, and he'd always take her side. He was too tired from work to deal with this mess. He never asked us what was going on. He never asked for our side. He never got down on one knee and talked with me. Never.

CHAPTER SEVEN

THE TEEN YEARS

I suppose I was not much different than the average teenager. There were the usual hormones and puberty to deal with. There was trying to figure out who I was and what I wanted to do growing up. But in the midst of all of that, I lived at the end of an isolated dirt road where no neighbors heard the yelling and screaming of our household. And those dark truths were kept that way out of fear.

The Woodinville house was on an acre of land surrounded by big cedar trees, mossy covered vine maples and rolling hills drenched thick with swarms of blackberries. We had our own well, and the property butted up against a large greenbelt and swamp. The only time anyone came driving down our long dark driveway was because they took a wrong turn or wanted to see what was at the end of the road.

When we first moved in, there was dark walnut paneling throughout the house and the living room had orange and black shag carpet. It was a dark house of brown on the outside as well as the inside. Not much sunshine made its way into that sunken spot at the end of the road. Half the property was covered in blackberries to the side of the house, the carport was just off the front door, and the well-house was smack in the middle of the front yard. The backyard slowly sloped into the swamp and into the greenbelt. I adventured occasionally back there when it was in the dry months of Washington, and found a really old cedar once, so large it was at least 20 feet in diameter. I wonder how many years old it was and what it had withstood and had witnessed in these woods. What had it heard I wondered? Did it hear the echoes of our own house?

Finally not being on the move, I was able to set some roots in at school and make friends. But my friends always seemed like they were surface friends. There was no one I ever told about the truths of what happened at my house. Candice was my next best friend and I spent many days playing and hanging out at her house. She was Canadian too, and our birthdays were just a month apart; we were destined to be besties. Throughout Junior High I had a few more "seizures" but by High School they had disappeared. All my seizures always happened when Karen was yelling at me: when I was under huge emotional stress.

I finished at Leota Junior High with some good memories too. Like Mr. Crosby and air-sports where we got to make model airplanes. I loved the sciences and felt certain I'd be a geophysicist someday. I loved tracking earthquakes and volcanoes and collecting all sorts of rocks and categorizing them. I also continued to play oboe for those three junior high years. While most girls were beginning to "blossom," I wasn't. I stopped growing at ninth grade and was just simply proud to make it to five feet. By now I also had acquired the need for glasses. I hated them. It just caused more teasing by some. But for the most part, life at school was settling down and I felt a growing sense of confidence by having friends, good grades, and curricular activities like band and crafts.

There were two times where I earned the wrath of Karen at school though. One was in health class where the teacher taught us about how the liver was a filter for all the bad stuff in our bodies. Well, we had liver as a weekly meal in my house; it was cheap. I told Karen how gross that was and unhealthy. She proceeded to march down to the school the next day and publically yell at the health teacher about his lack of knowledge on how healthy it is to eat such a high source of iron. She did this in front of the entire class. I was embarrassed beyond belief, not only by her actions, but also that kids now knew that I ate liver at home.

Another time I earned her disapproval was when I needed to override a requirement in my classes. I was supposed to take Home-Ec, but it would stop me from doing band. I got approval to have the Home-Ec excused by the school counselor. Karen was furious about Home-Ec being removed from my schedule. So instead she took it upon herself to teach me at home. That led to the next several years at home being extremely stressful in all areas of cooking and sewing. Karen was a perfectionist and ruled by her way was the only way. She would lose her temper quickly and begin to yell at any error. And when the errors continued, she would then try to psychoanalyze me asking what I was preoccupied with and what was troubling me. Of course I could never tell her that the trouble was *her*!

The routine in the kitchen was she'd ask me to make a meal for supper, however she would hover and watch every step I did. She would bark orders and correct me if I made an error, didn't do things fast enough, fine enough, or clean enough. Her presence alone made me extremely nervous, and when one is nervous, they don't function at their highest ability. That was me. I would freeze. I would panic. I'd begin to make stupid mistakes, causing her to get even angrier with me and my "stupidity." After enough attempts to fix it and make it her way, I'd be like a timid mouse scared frozen. That's when she would dive in on her attempt to be a psychiatrist and analyze. She shut everything down in the kitchen after she'd finally had enough and slapped me across the face in her attempt to "wake me up" and get into shape. When physical violence didn't work and I was a crumpled pile on the floor, she'd then attempt to be the psychiatrist, calm and gentle. Of course nothing was wrong, but she insisted something was.

I usually started by lying and saying I was stressed about a class. But she wouldn't buy it. So I'd lie to the next layer in an attempt to appease her inquiry, and say it was a disagreement between my sister and me or a friend. But she didn't usually buy that one either. Finally, I had to lie at the deepest level, and say I was troubled by a memory of Real Mom in Canada and some made-up abuse story she had done. Now Karen was happy with my answer, would address it with a psychiatrist answer of degrading Real Mom, and let me off the hook for my inadequacies in the kitchen. This usually took about 1–2 hours.

The same would happen with a sewing instruction from her. I always felt like I was walking on eggshells, always doing things wrong: No, always doing *everything* wrong.

Karen would wax and wane between picking on my sister and picking on me in this method. But one thing was consistent: we were not the perfect children she had wanted. We were broken. We would always be broken. During this time, as my sister blossomed into her female body, and I did not, I was being groomed to believe I was ugly. My parents would regularly compliment my sister on how beautiful she was growing to be, how she could be a model, but never spoke words of affirmation to my flat chested appearance. The lack of words can be just as damaging to the soul as words of harm. And so I began to believe I was ugly and no one would ever think me beautiful or want me. Karen definitely didn't act like she wanted me.

I had plenty of crushes in high school, but never dated until my senior year. By then I had learned how to have an identity as a runner and band geek. But there was a reverence in these identities. Being the oboe player in multiple bands and the orchestra at school gave me a positive identity and plenty of affirmation. Being in the top of the runners for Cross-Country and Track also came with its perks, when hearing your name listed over the school intercom for successes in the day's before meets. But no one asked me out on a date or to be their girlfriend or to dances. So, I thought, I must be ugly. So I came to the conclusion in my high school years to focus on my running and academics, as this is what people liked about me. In these areas I could be affirmed and I could please people. I could even please Karen. By my junior year of high school I had made it all the way to the national levels in track. Karen seemed proud to have me as her daughter. So I focused on doing above and beyond in these areas. Eventually though, I learned that I was doing everything for others, being a people-pleaser, and was not doing these activities for my own enjoyment. Soon injuries happened from sprained ankles and stress fractures. I was once again, not something Karen seemed proud of. I was not only ugly now, but also a let-down and a failure.

By the end of high school, I had grown close to another friend, Jen. She was Mormon and her family was very nice. My family had stopped going to church regularly, and I went by myself to the First Lutheran Church in Bothell. I enjoyed helping out with Vacation Bible School during the summer and helped lead the music program. But I was also lonely there, as my friends from school didn't go to that church or any church at all. With Karen being Methodist, and Dad being Catholic, they had settled on Lutheran when we lived in Canada. When we moved to the states, we started going to the Methodist church in Monroe because Karen wanted her son to be baptized Methodist. Once he was born and baptized, we returned to the Lutheran church in Bothell. But eventually, they all stopped going. Mostly after my sister was kicked out.

My sister turned 18 in February, and by then things were of a super high stress load between Karen and her. They regularly fought, and my sister never held her tongue as I had learned to do. She would raise her voice back and get hit across the face. But she took it. She was bigger now. She was the same size as Karen, I was not, and never would be. One argument, my sister said she was finally going to leave, she'd had enough. Karen said, "Fine, go!"

As my sister began to pack up her things and walk out the front door, Karen stopped her.

"Where do you think you are going with my stuff?!" she yelled at her.

"I'm only taking my stuff. Nothing here in my bags are yours," my sister snapped back.

"Everything you have and everything you are wearing I bought, and so they are mine," Karen retorted. "You're not leaving with any of that. It's mine. If you want to leave, you leave with nothing."

Karen had her strip down naked on the front steps of our home and stand there at the age of 17 to make the point that everything we had was because of Karen, and we truly had nothing without her. This was a sobering thought. After that, Karen convinced Dad that my sister should move out when she turned 18. This was still during her senior year of high school. My sister and I both babysat the neighbor's children, and once we turned 16 we had regular paying jobs. My sister worked at the Dairy Queen in Woodinville, and I worked at the local Albertsons grocery store. Karen managed our paychecks and made sure we put 75% into the savings account we each had.

So my sister moved out when she turned 18 in the middle of her senior high school year with some friends from the prior year of school, into an apartment. She worked the night shift at the gas station in town and finished high school. Karen had made her point clear; her duties in parenting and taking care of another women's child were done when they turned 18. I think deep down Karen wanted my sister to fail on her own and come back crawling and begging to be taken back. That would have given Karen the biggest sense of pride and accomplishment all in her twisted way. But my sister was stubborn in her own way too. She graduated and that summer signed up for the US Army, as the alternative of returning home was not a viable option for her. So, off she went, and alone I dealt with the continued wrath of Karen.

Before my sister moved out, and had been living at home those last years, Dad and I would hang out in the carport which now had been turned into a garage, and worked on the vehicles, doing oil changes, engine swap outs, and general tune-ups and care. We'd hear the yelling and screaming in the house, the occasional crashing of dishes. Sometimes Dad would pause as I handed him a 3/8" wrench for the engine we were working on, but he'd never stop and go in and check what was going on. To check and see if everyone was okay. We both had an unspoken understanding between us that it was safer for both of us to stay outside in the garage. Keep low, and stay out of it.

I was so thankful for those weekends with Dad in the garage. Not only did I learn a lot about engines, I also got to know my father. I knew the mixture of Dad's smell of sweat with the grease and oils of the vehicles. I learned he was a patient teacher. When I messed up in the beginning in finding the right size of wrench which he called for, he didn't bark, curse, belittle or swear at me. He would share stories of himself as a child, how he had believed he was superman, tied a towel around his neck, and jumped off Grandma's back porch into the rock garden below. There was the story about when she was sick with cancer, and he was trying to make a cake for her to cheer her up in bed, and the recipe called for egg whites, but all they had was brown farm chicken eggs, so he went in and cried his failure to his mother, which brought her to laughter nonetheless. He shared about being accidentally struck in his chin by his brother swinging a double headed axe on the farm, because he stood too close to his backward swing behind him. He shared how him and his brothers set up a train set on the dining room table and would pass the condiments by placing them on the train cars. He shared stories of his adventures at the logging camps and the outdoors. He seemed so happy talking about some of those memories, especially the ones of canoeing on the Northern Interior Canadian Lakes. I loved hearing his stories. Hearing his laugh. Seeing him smile again. I loved being able to complete projects with him. It was our sacred time together. It was as if the world stood still when we were out there. We could spend 6-8 hours, and I would be completely satisfied. And he seemed happy out there too. It was better than being inside with the rage and wrath of Karen.

After my sister left, Dad and I became Karen's remaining targets. I was sixteen, and by then weekly encounters of arguments were normal. My brother was only five then. I wonder how much he remembers. After my sister moved out, I got her bedroom, and I no longer shared a room with my little brother. As a blossoming sixteen-year-old, it was awkward sharing a bedroom with a five-year-old boy. So, I got my own room, the one closest to the kitchen, and farthest from my brother's and parent's rooms at the end of the hallway. Being situated closest to the living room and kitchen meant I unfortunately heard all their arguments though. Most times, it was the same stuff, but one night will always stick out to me.

It was another one of those nights. I laid awake in bed, listening to the arguing, and the constant swearing. The dishes broke just as easily as the jagged words were thrown. This night wasn't't much different from the hundreds of others I had listened to. It had become a weekly routine by the time I was sixteen. Sometimes it was more often, sometimes, there was peace for a month. It always started the same way—"The children are putting a wedge between you and me," she would scream. Karen would curse and swear, accusing my father that his allegiance to his children was stronger than to his wife—which in her opinion was just plain wrong. He never really argued back, and he rarely ever raised his voice in return. She would hit and throw things at him, and yet he never dished it back. At least from my vantage point, lying frozen in my bed, waiting for the peace, so I could finally get some sleep before school began the next day.

Usually the arguments would end with her taking it too far by bringing my father's dead mother into the argument, stating that he never had a real mother, due to her drinking away the cancer pain.

"What do you know about what a family is supposed to be like? Your father committed suicide and your mother was a drunk because she couldn't't deal with the pain of cancer."

When those words were spoken, Dad would always respond back in a quavering, almost inaudible voice, "Damn you—you didn't have to go there. Damn you."

Soon I'd hear the front door open and slam. Then the car's engine would start up in the driveway, as Karen would open the front door only to antagonize him more by yelling, "go ahead—run away!" Dad would peel out of the driveway. The house would be silent, but the tension was still there. For the next couple of hours I would lay there breathless, and awake. Wide awake.

You would think after all those hundreds of arguments like this; the routine wouldn't get to me. I'd lie there, and he'd always return. But I never knew for sure. I had my doubts—constant doubts. The fear a young child has of being left stranded, alone in a dark scary room was the suffocating emotion that weighed over me. There was that constant doubt that this time, was the last time. This was it—he'd had enough. He'd never return. Not unless I prayed. It may sound like such a naive and childish thing to do, but I felt a security in those moments of conversing with the Lord. I would talk to God, asking—no—pleading for my father to return to me.

"Please let him know and remember who he's left behind . . . .me . . . with her . . . please don't let him forget I'm here. Please make him come back".

The idea of him being gone forever was too painful. I always felt that if I didn't plead, that my father wouldn't get the messages, and he wouldn't return. Then I would hear the car drive back down the gravel driveway and the front door of the house would open slowly and quietly, hours later, and I knew he was home. Then I could breathe. I literally would let out a deep sigh—it worked—prayers are answered is what I thought. Karen was in bed, and he would join her quietly, and the house would be still again. Not a sound. Peace. Peace as I knew it at the time.

Tonight was a different night though. Usually after a few hours of arguing and the normal routine of dishes and furniture being broken, words of an array being flung, Dad would leave. The words were different tonight—they were harsher. There was a different "presence" in the air and I could feel this "thing" but couldn't describe it, but there was something different happening tonight in the house.

I heard the mention of the set of rifles in their bedroom closet. My heart stopped. The next thing I heard was them running to the bedroom—a violent and frantic race. Through the massive bumping down the hallway, the loud, harsh words continued. Doors opened and slammed. I heard a struggle, I heard crying. I lay paralyzed, not knowing what to do—or even if I should or could do anything. I waited and listened.

This night was different; Dad didn't leave. He did something much different. He stood his ground and said no more. Of course, like most who have been abused and stay in the presence of their abuser, the initial energy to stand one's ground is undercut by staying in relationship with the abuser. And so it was with Dad. For a couple weeks after him taking his stand, Karen was the one to walk around on egg shells. She was quiet. She didn't argue or raise her voice. But then old routines returned, and Dad and I found ourselves in her path of rage and wrath again.

I tried to spend a lot more time at my friend Jen's house after my sister moved out. It provided peace and calm, and a glimpse of what a normal family was. They didn't yell at each other. They were kind and respectful. Her mom didn't raise her voice at her husband or throw dishes and break furniture. All six children had chores and they did them. There was family game night. It was such a complete one-eighty from what I experienced at my home. So it was no surprise that I became intrigued and interested in how they lived so peacefully together. Before the end of my senior year, I was attending church services with Jen and her family at their Mormon church. I didn't really understand that there were differences in religions or what theology was. I just knew this provided the ground rules for peace in a family and it worked. My family didn't seem to have any ground rules, and yet we were Christian. Karen quoted the bible all the time when she yelled and screamed at me, but it didn't change her behaviors.

I turned eighteen on June 7, 1992, graduated from high school a week later, and a week after that became homeless. Many believe being homeless is being out on the streets. And that is true. But being homeless is also couch-surfing or simply not being able to live at home anymore. I had been accepted to Central Washington University in Ellensburg and even had a roommate ready to move with into the dorms in the fall. But all that went out the window in one night of Karen's rage. Maybe it was just a great excuse for her to get rid of another eighteen-year-old child that wasn't her own. I don't know. I had been promised their full support financially for college just as my sister had. As with her, I also now had nothing. And what monies had been in my account from my years of work and savings, just like my sister's, were also non-existent.

How did I become homeless? Because I uttered the words that I wanted to be baptized Mormon. There was no discussion. Period. I had become a devil worshipper and a cult member according to Karen. I was lost to them. She would not allow me in her home ever again if I was a Mormon, she screamed at me. I was allowed a simple bag of my clothes, and was told to go. I was officially homeless. Dad drove me in silence to Jen's house. That became my home for the next several months. They accepted me in, where my own family had failed to. I hadn't even been baptized Mormon, and yet, I was cast out on my own. Is this how Christians treat others? What happened to love one another; even love your enemy?

So I began the next season of my life, on my own.

CHAPTER EIGHT

ON MY OWN

Jen's family was caring and nice, and they welcomed me fully into their family. I left my job at Albertson's and got a fulltime job closer to where they lived in Kirkland at the Drug Emporium. I worked my way quickly from cashier to manager in a matter of months. During this time I began taking the missionary discussions to be baptized. I still didn't comprehend the theology or differences between my Lutheran practices and Mormons. They used the same Bible I had grown up with, but had a few other scriptures too. All I knew and understood was this faith practiced what it preached: peace in the family. And that was something I wanted desperately.

Sometime in July I got baptized. I also applied for attendance at BYU and was accepted. I thought I was back on track to going to college and carrying on with my life. But there was not the finances for college. Dad and Karen would not give one cent which they promised for my college because it would be going to "that cult." So I didn't go to school in the fall. I stayed living with Jen's family for almost nine months, never hearing a word from my own family.

Finally, that winter, Jen's family tried to mediate some reconciliation between me and my parents. My parents agreed to allow me to move back home, but I still wasn't allowed in the house. I could live in the old camper set back up the hill amongst the blackberry bushes on the property. Dad hooked up a propane tank for cooking, a garden hose for water, and an electrical extension cord for heat and electricity. I was allowed to come in to the main house to use the shower and bathroom, but I was not to interact with my little brother and influence him in anyway. I was merely a guest on their property. I had to stock my own cupboards and utensils.

When they kicked me out of the house previously, they took and sold my car. It had been an old yellow Datsun 280z that Dad and I found in a farmer's field and bought for $200. We fixed it up, and I paid for all my gas and car insurance. But it wasn't legally mine, so I lost that too when I was kicked out. Once again, like my sister stripped naked, I had nothing that hadn't come from them. So I had no transportation, hence why I changed jobs when living with Jen's family. Now I was back to needing a new job again, and a vehicle. I had some money saved up, and so Dad helped me find a used 1980 little baby blue Ford Escort hatchback. We were back in the garage getting the car all fixed up just like old times. We never spoke about the church or what had happened. He simply followed the orders Karen gave and kept the peace.

By May I had landed a job with Great Western Bank located in Bellevue in the loan department, processing loan papers. Between moving in to the camper, which I found out was infested with ants, buying a car, and being placed at a new job, my bank funds diminished greatly. I eventually was so limited with funds that my meals were comprised of mixed flour and water together to make pancakes in the camper.

I was never invited to meals at the house with my family. I was no longer treated as family. Karen rarely spoke to me, and when she did, it was to undercut everything I was doing with my life. Nothing was good in her eyes that I was doing. I was a devil worshipper and part of a cult. She made it very clear she wanted me off her property as soon as possible.

During my time with Jen, she had me attend social functions at the church where I got to meet some boys. Some I recognized from high school, so it was nice to get back into friends again despite the emotional turmoil of the exile treatment of my family. One young man was Brandon. He had graduated with Jen and me from Woodinville High School and now worked with the Men's Warehouse suit company. He invited me to his company Christmas party at a fancy hotel in Seattle that year. Brandon had light brown hair. His eyes were set deeply into his head, giving him pronounced eyebrows. He was five foot nine and solidly built. Brandon drove a white 1979 Porsche 926 with black leather interior. His family was more financially well off than mine. Unfortunately, it snowed on that first date of ours to his company Christmas party and his car didn't make it but a few blocks from his parent's home before it slid into the ditch. There was no damage to his car, but boy did he get angry and upset. I was used to being around upset angry people most of my life, so I knew to stay quiet and stay out of the way until they let off some steam. His dad came and got us out of the ditch and we carried onto the party. It was a wonderful evening.

I went on a double date with Brandon and Jen and her boyfriend later that spring. Brandon asked me to marry him sometime in late May. It all happened rather fast. I told my parents about this development, and once again, that threw Karen into a rage. I was asked to leave the property and get my own place. I needed to live on my own before getting married. I was too young to get married at nineteen. I had only been on one date alone with this young man. Once again, they were disappointed and furious with my decisions. I had failed them again.

So I moved into a studio apartment in Snohomish with a co-worker from the bank. It was all one room, just the basic kitchen and our two beds. The bathroom was off to the back of the apartment. It was an old historical mansion along the main street in Snohomish which had been subdivided into multiple apartments. We were on the bottom floor. We had brick walls and floors. It wasn't much, but it was a step up from an ant infested camper and watered floured pancakes. I was now fully on my own, and I was so proud of myself!

I was so caught up in the euphoria that a young man actually liked me and wanted to marry me that I didn't really pay much attention to what this reality meant. I was a naive young woman with little self-esteem. I truly believed that if I didn't jump on this proposal, no other would come along. After all, I was ugly and unwanted. As the summer came, Brandon was sent off to Basic Training for the Army Reserves which he had just signed up for. After Basic, he was sent onto his specialty training as a German linguist interrogator at Fort Ord in California. We went on a total of three dates that summer before we got married September 4th. We had plenty of phone conversations though, which unfortunately left me a very high phone bill.

Sometimes when he called from the barracks he was drunk. One time he thought I was another girl from our high school whom he had a crush on, and I learned what he really wanted in a girl.

So being the people pleasing person I had been formed to be in an abusive home, I now continued that attitude into my marriage with Brandon. Do anything and everything to keep the peace and keep him happy. I dyed my hair blonde to look like her. I became so overly anxious about everything in keeping him happy, I lost an unhealthy amount of weight and was only one hundred pounds. But sometimes no matter what you do, you can't be another person's happiness. It's just that simple.

On our wedding day at the Mormon Church, Jen's mom and Brandon's mom got into an argument. Dad and Karen attended the wedding too, but Karen was visibly not happy about being there. We had our high school friends attend too. Some friends had decorated my blue Ford Escort in whipping cream on the windows with words of blessings and congratulations, and there were tin cans tied to the back bumper. It should have been a joyous day. But people with anger issues can only keep up the façade for so long.

I unknowingly had no windshield washer fluid in my car that day, and as Brandon and I hopped in the car to drive off from the wedding amongst cheers of happiness, he turned on the wipers to clear off the whipping cream words. Everything smeared and nothing washed clean. His anger exploded like nothing I had never seen before. He was angry at the car. He was angry at me. He pounded on the steering wheel. He swore. He hit the back of my seat. This was my husband on our wedding day. It should have been a joyous day. But cycles continue.

We made it the couple miles to his parent's house. By then I was in tears. He continued to swear at me over my ineptness. I went inside to change out of my big white wedding dress. He stayed outside and washed the car in his tux with the garden hose all the while still loudly yelling and cursing. He finally came inside to change. He calmed down and apologized for his behavior and said he'd never act that way again. His parents and sister came home shortly after, and we packed our overnight bags for our one-night honeymoon at a local hotel suite his parents had gotten us. I honestly don't even remember that night. I was still in such shock over the car that I think I was numb. What had I done? What and who had I married?

The next morning we returned to his parents' house and opened wedding gifts. We packed up my little baby blue Ford Escort with all my belongings and the wedding gifts, filled the windshield wiper fluid, and began our drive down to Fort Ord, California. I was officially married at nineteen to a man after three dates, who obviously had an anger issue that I had not fully comprehended before now. I was going thousands of miles away from family and friends, not knowing anyone, and being fully dependent on this man.

Dear Lord, what had I gotten myself into?

CHAPTER NINE

REPEAT

We got married on Labor Day weekend 1993. It allowed the necessary time for him to take leave to get married and drive back down with me. As a military wife, there are forms and identification badges to acquire. I had to learn my way around this new form of life. Brandon of course assisted in driving me around and showing me where the Commissary was, where his office was, and where the beach was. As long as I knew how to get to those places and our studio apartment everything would be just fine.

The Monterey Bay area is a beautiful place. Ford Ord sits just north and east of it. Seaside, California, is the closest town and is mostly occupied by the sand dunes of the Pacific Ocean. Ford Ord was a dry and hot place with the Laguna Seca raceway set on its back door. There were nights where we could hear the cars racing around the track from our studio window.

Our apartment was on the lower level of the mission style apartment complex. It had stucco exterior with nice paved walkways throughout. The apartment was "fully furnished," which meant that it had a futon that folded out to be our bed. There was a small half counter to separate the living room/bedroom from the kitchen. Off the kitchen was a small bathroom and a hallway closet. There was one window in the front bedroom/

living room. The total space was 650 square feet, smaller than the trailer I had grown up in. I had dishes and pots, and with the addition of the wedding gifts, we were set. We lived simply. Brandon had a military stipend for being married which allowed us to live in the apartment on base, but we still needed a second income. I had put in a transfer with the bank to get a job in California, but they did not have an opening at the loan department, only as a teller. I wasn't going to be fussy, so I took the job.

It wasn't much different than being a cashier at Drug Emporium, except now I was dealing with larger amounts of cash and transactions. I quickly learned the necessary steps and fit in well. Every Friday seemed to be our busiest. Somewhere it was a payday for someone it seemed. One particular gentleman would come in every Friday to do his banking business. He was an older man, and the years had not been kind to him. His aged faced, and his homeless smell, announced his situation clearly. He often mumbled to himself, yet he was harmless, but it was evident he had been harmed by the world and how it had treated him. He would approach the counter and dig out of his pocket a fist full of one dollar bills. Most people when counting money would sometimes lick a finger and then use the dampness of that fingertip to help grab the paper and separate it from the others. This gentleman had it slightly backwards; he would lick each bill with his tongue then grab it with his other hand before counting it onto the counter in front of us. We each were kind to him, deposited his money into his account, bid him nicely farewell, and then put on gloves to pick up the cash. If one could wash money, these were the bills that needed it most.

After three months as a teller, a loan processor position in the neighboring town of Salinas became available, and I applied. I got the job. My new co-workers were wonderful to work with, very positive and friendly. I was an adult now, and all the bullying which I had experienced as a kid didn't follow me here. It was so nice. We all got along so well. It was so peaceful and sunny in California. But it wasn't so peaceful at home in the little 650 square foot studio apartment.

Although he was Mormon, Brandon is what many would call a "Jack-Mormon"—one who goes to church on Sunday, but then lives a completely different life the rest of the week. He learned this way of living from his mother, who would go to church in the morning, and by afternoon was smoking her cigarettes (something forbidden by the church). Brandon would go out drinking with his captain and military buddies regularly. This didn't help his anger episodes. We couldn't afford eating out, so I cooked most our meals and we ate on our futon watching TV, as we didn't have a dining room nor dining room table.

I had developed a clicking in my jaw as a teenager every time I ate. Karen had taken me to the dentist, who then sent us to the orthodontist who highly recommended braces. I had oversized fang looking eye teeth and overcrowding. When the orthodontist told Karen I desperately needed braces to get rid of the painful clicking and locking of my jaw, she looked at me, and in front of the doctor, asked if I could still chew my food. Which I answered meekly "yes." She stormed us out of his office stating I obviously didn't need braces to eat right and would be just fine as I was. Well, since all our dates prior to marriage had been out at restaurants, we had never eaten in the silence of just the two of us alone. Brandon had never heard my clicking jaw before; my TMJ. He became so disgusted with it that I was forced to eat all my meals in the bathroom when he was home, while he sat and watched TV in the other room. I hated eating and being excluded; being treated as lesser than, as an ugly deformed person. Unaccepted. Unwanted.

Brandon made known his displeasure with me regularly. It didn't take much to get him upset. He was just like Karen. Exactly like Karen. It could be a simple look which he took wrong. It could be the way I walked or swallowed. It could be the way I made noise in the kitchen washing dishes, or how there wasn't enough milk in the fridge. It could be as simple as the outfit I was wearing. His anger was explosive and loud.

About a month after our wedding he had a back injury and required surgery up at the San Jose Naval Hospital. The surgery was several hours long, and he didn't stay long in the hospital until they released him for home care. Now I was in charge of caring for him in all aspects. Where he showed no care or empathy for me, I was now to do for him. Of course I did it. From helping walk around and being his crutch to and from the bathroom and in and out of the shower and getting dressed. Driving him to and from physical therapy appointments and follow up doctor appointments all the way up in San Jose. I did it all, and without any disregard for his continued anger towards me.

When we went back to Washington to his parents' house for Christmas, he was healed and back to work. I'll never forget his father dropping us off at the airport to return to California, and him turning to his son, grabbing him by the shoulders and saying, "take care of her." I had an instant fondness in that moment towards his father. I wondered if he knew what was going on in our home in California. Did he know of his son's anger issues and violent tendencies? "

"Take care of her" his father had said. I had never heard someone speak that about me. I was always the one taking care of others. Always the one taking care to not be the center of anyone's attention, staying out of the way, and especially those who had anger issues. Yes, I needed caring, but who would do it?

After Brandon's year down in California was completed, he was released from training, and put on simple month reserve duties. We moved back to Washington and lived with his family for a couple of months before we found our own place. Almost exactly a year after our wedding, I began having extreme abdominal pain. His mother thought I was pregnant, but I had been told to get on the pill by her the month before our wedding.

It turned out that I had two huge ovarian cysts; one the size of a small honeydew melon and one the size of an orange. The surgeon wasn't sure he could save both ovaries. I came out of surgery with both ovaries intact and felt blessed. Shortly after, Brandon and I moved out of his folks' place and into a little condo of our own in the Renton Highlands. His parents helped co-sign to get us started. I was able to get a job as a teller with Seafirst Bank nearby, and Brandon got a job at the local auto parts store. We adopted two little miniature-Schnauzer-Pomeranian mixed puppies. Both female; one we named Raisin (that became his), and one named Brandi (which became predominantly mine). I believed for a moment that life back near home was going to make him happy and not so angry, but that was not the case. I thought the dogs would bring joy to our home, but that was not the case.

We needed to live meagerly, but Brandon also loved to live beyond his means, believing that if there were checks in the checkbook, there was money in the account. I took on a second job at the local McDonalds. I worked the bank 9am-6pm, and then McDonalds from 8pm-midnight. Brandon attempted to go to college. Before long, the financial challenges overtook us, and we could not pay rent. His anger and frustration grew over why he wasn't able to live like he wanted to. His anger was focused on me. Although we were good attending Mormons, even having gone through the temple by then, it didn't change his behaviors.

One night his anger and continued violence got out of hand and he pinned me against the wall while yelling at me and bit my nose. I had already encountered his passive aggressive behavior in California where he would trip me or push me down a flight of stairs at the apartment complex where I'd get twisted ankles and bruises, or use walls and doors to cause his harm. Claiming me klutzy and not coordinated to others. But he had not yet actually struck me. This was the first where he himself actually caused the harm to me. Not the stairs, not the slammed door on my hand or my head. I called the bishop to come over, as I couldn't take this anymore. We needed intervention.

The bishop came over immediately that night and talked to him. He told Brandon he couldn't behave like this, and then told me to be on my best behavior. That was all. He left and asked to be called if it happened again. We ended up moving to a double-wide trailer out in Auburn shortly after due to our failed finances.

It was during this time, that Brandon was called up for a several week military reserve exercise overseas. About a month after he left, I found out I was pregnant. Ever since the ovarian cyst surgery, I had been forced to be on the pill to stop any more cysts from growing. I ended up doing a cycle of three months on the pill and three months off the pill as we attempted to get pregnant.

As a young Mormon couple, we were expected to start having children by this time in our marriage. So I continued this routine of three months on, and three months off the pill. But finally, I became pregnant that summer of 1996. He was ecstatic. His family was happy to have their first grandchild, and Karen actually wanted to be a part of our lives now. Pregnancy didn't stop his anger, and it was foolish to think having a child would make him behave better.

Two weeks after my daughter was born, I knew I'd be needing to protect her for the rest our lives around him. She was all strapped up in her car seat to be carried out to the car for her post-delivery check-up, but was beginning to get fussy and began to cry. As she sat in her car seat on the couch, and I was putting on my shoes at the front door, Brandon walked over to her, and placed his face inches from hers.

"SHUT THE FUCK UP!" he screamed at the top of his voice.

I was terrified. She stopped crying immediately and had a frozen blank face for at least an hour after that. No emotion from her. Nothing. He carried her to the car and we went to the post-delivery appointment. Everything checked out. She was fine. But she wasn't fine. We'd never be fine. And I knew it. And there was nothing I could do about it. There was no one I could say anything to. She was frozen and so was I.

A few months later, and having financial problems again, we were forced to move into my parent's place this time. Karen still didn't like us being in the same house because we were Mormon, but she also didn't want to lose the chance to be around her granddaughter. So she had Dad build walls and a door in the house to make two separate living quarters. By then the construction of the addition onto the house had been completed, leaving the original bedrooms and what had been the front living room and entrance to us, while my parents and younger brother lived in the new section of the house with the kitchen, front entryway and upstairs bedrooms. We got a hot plate and Dad built a counter top in the living room for us to cook on. We washed our dishes in the bathroom. I took our laundry to the laundromat. It truly was living separately like Karen wanted. My brother was in elementary school and she didn't want our "cult-like religion" affecting him. My daughter took her first steps in this setting when she was nine months old. Her brother was also conceived there during marital-rape. Years later, Dad told me he heard my screams that night and Brandon's anger on the other side of the wall in the house and wanted to intercede, but Karen told him it was our marriage and to stay out of it. What would have happened if he had come to our side of the house? I wonder. I truly wonder.

CHAPTER TEN

CHILDREN

Some children are made out of love. Some are not. It was not a joyous night when my son was conceived. Brandon wanted what he wanted; it didn't matter that I said no. It didn't matter that he held me down amidst my struggles, cries and screams. Afterwards, I cried at him to leave. I was officially done. He had never treated me like this before. He had progressed in his physical violence, but he had never forced himself like this before. I was retching inside. I told him to leave again. He apologized and said he didn't know why he had done that. He was profusely apologetic; but I had seen and heard those same words when he had been angry before and hurtful. Those words of apology never seemed to change his future behavior from repeating the same acts. I wasn't going to have him do this again to me.

"Leave, now!" I said again, this time raising my voice. He asked where he was supposed to go.

"I don't care. Just leave. Go live with your parents. I don't want to see you ever again." His parents only lived 15 minutes away. He left. I cried that whole night. I knew my timing, and I already knew this was going to be another pregnancy.

In the morning his parents called. I don't know if he confessed that he had raped me, or if he told them we had an argument and I had told him to leave. His mom wanted me to come over and talk it out. So I went over.

We all sat in the living room of their house, his parents on one side of the room, Brandon and I on the other side, but not sitting next to each other. He sat in one arm chair and I sat in another. Brandon's father was silent, but his mother had plenty to say to me. Somehow it all came to a head where she was in my face yelling at me, just like Karen. I sat there silently, realizing this was the person Brandon had learned his anger from. She yelled at me about my duties of a wife and proper treatment of a husband. I held up my hand as a stop sign and interrupted her, and not having learned my lesson from Karen, I repeated what I had said in this same situation years earlier.

"I'll speak to you when you're ready to calm down and talk like an adult." I said.

In a flash she attacked me with her long-nailed hands, striking my face and scratching me and ripping out my right earring. As quickly as she attacked me over my calm words, the men in the room each took their sides and placed themselves between us. Brandon's dad said it was time for us to leave, while he tried to calm down his wife. Meanwhile, Brandon yelled at his mother for her behavior, but placed his arm around me in protection and got me out of her reach and out of the living room. We left. I never found my earring and it was never returned to me either. It was my favorite turtle earring.

When we arrived back at my parent's house, I immediately went to their side of the house and told them what happened and got the blood off my face and cleaned up. Dad was furious and wanted to press charges. I said no, and took the blame that I probably shouldn't have been so flippant in what I said. I made it like I was to blame; it was my fault I got attacked. Just like a domestic violence victim does. I had already been hearing for years how a black eye or a bloodied lip was my fault, first from Karen then from Brandon; why should this time be any different. When you hear the phrase, "look what you made me do" time and again, you begin to believe it. And so, I did.

It wasn't long until the pregnancy was confirmed. When I told Brandon, his response was, "well, get an abortion then and get rid of it."

"No. How could you say such a thing?"

"Get rid of it or I will" he said sternly.

So I scheduled an abortion with my health care provider. They were allowed in the first ten weeks of a pregnancy. As I waited for the appointment to arrive, my heart weighed heavy. Every fiber in my body told me this was wrong. I was killing a child. How could I do this? I looked at my daughter and the love I had for her. How could I not love this new child the same? It was after all, MY child. I had to make a choice.

The week of the scheduled abortion, I called and canceled my appointment. Brandon was furious. We were already financially strapped and living with my parents; how could we afford another child?

"It's my child, my body, and I'm not going to kill this child!" I said. "You made this child, and you are going to learn to handle the consequences of your actions."

This small exchange, turned him into a rage. "How dare you speak to me like that!"

And in an instance before I knew what hit me, he punched my stomach hard. I dropped to the floor and he kicked me several times in the stomach.

"If you won't take care of it, I will" he shouted as he kicked me.

My son was born that summer. He wasn't breathing when he was born. He was a two on the Apgar score test, but he pulled through. Both my children were only 15 months apart, and I knew it would be a struggle to juggle two little ones, but they were my greatest joy.

While I was pregnant with my son, we moved out of my parent's and into a rental house in Federal Way. Finances were good again. Brandon had gotten a new job with a small family owned company in Issaquah learning and using CAD (Computer Added Drafting). I was still working for the bank, but after my daughter's birth had switched out of being a teller and into ATM processing in the evenings in downtown Seattle. This allowed for Brandon to work during the days and me at nights. I would drive to his office with the children in their car seats, and switch everything over to his car, and he would drive home with them, while I drove into Seattle for my night shift until 1am. I really never knew what took place in the evenings at home while I was at work, but I constantly prayed for their safety.

Brandon's anger went in waves. Sometimes he would tell me how "out of control the children would cry" the whole drive home and he didn't know what to do with them. How he couldn't handle it any more. He began smoking to help handle his stress, and I couldn't stand the smell of it. I demanded that he never smoke around the children and he followed it when I was around on the weekends. But his hands would stink of the cigarettes and I became bolder, demanding he wash his hands before touching them. Slowly, I was finding my voice.

Usually I would make it home just in time for the middle-of-the-night feeding. So, I would take the babies to the living room at the other end of the house, the farthest away from him possible, and I would snuggle with my babies on the couch and fall asleep together as I fed them their bottles or breast fed the youngest. My daughter was almost 17 months old and my son was just a couple of months old. It was a peaceful time for the most part. Brandon and I rarely slept in the same bed anymore, because of my night schedule and the feeding of the kids. It was the weekends I had to worry about; when we were both home and I got to see his temper rage.

I always stayed with the children. If I went grocery shopping on the weekend, they came with me. The only time they were alone with him was during the work week evenings. One Saturday afternoon, he had fallen asleep in the living room. The living room was an add-on to the small rambler house by the owner. They had converted the garage by putting up walls, installing windows and throwing down a carpet (without a pad below), to form the living room. The step down into the old garage still existed off of the laundry room. The kitchen and dining room linked the laundry room and the old garage to the rest of the house which had two other bedrooms. This carpeted converted garage into a living room was where the kids and I spent the most of our time. It got great sunshine and I had many of my plants here. The kid's toys were here too, as well as the TV.

Brandon, had fallen asleep, so I went into the kitchen to prepare supper. I checked in on the kids, saw him asleep on the couch, my daughter playing quietly with her toys, and my son asleep in his bouncy chair. I went back to the kitchen to complete supper. Soon I heard Brandon screaming at my daughter in one of his rages. I quickly ran to the living room, where at the same moment, I saw him standing and holding her, shaking her and then throwing her backwards onto the floor. The back of her head hit the unpadded carpeted floor with a loud smack. She was crying immediately. I ran to her and held her tightly.

"What's wrong with you??!!" I screamed at him.

His face was bright red, "look what she did!!!" he yelled. I hadn't noticed as I had rushed in, that there was dirt everywhere.

My daughter had taken handfuls of dirt from the potted plants and began building her own little imaginary garden plots throughout the room, which also included on top of him on the couch where he slept. He was furious. She was crying. Soon she began vomiting. I knew that crack sound on her head hitting the floor was not good. I comforted her as he stormed out of the room telling me to clean it up. I laid her on the couch and quickly scooped as much dirt off of the floor and couch and placed it back into the pots of plants. She continued to cry. By now my son was crying too.

I heard the back door slam shut behind Brandon and soon smelled his cigarette smoke leak into the house. I grabbed the vacuum and cleaned up the mess. Still she cried. She got sick again. I knew I needed to take her to the hospital right away. Brandon came back into the house calmer and apologized for erupting. I told him, I think she was hurt with a possible concussion and I needed to take her in to the hospital right away. He looked scared and worried. I'm not sure if it was for her health or for what he had done. He stayed home while I took our daughter to the Mary Bridge's Children's Hospital in Tacoma, Washington.

When I arrived at the hospital that evening, I was so scared for her. I knew something wasn't right. I had no idea what I was going to say to them. I had learned to easily lie about my own injuries, but how do I lie about a child's injuries? I told them she fell backwards on a hard floor which was essentially a carpeted cement floor. They did x-rays and checked her over. She had a mild concussion, but otherwise would be fine. They sent us back home with instructions to rest, but wake her up every couple of hours to check on her that night.

I was terrified they knew I was lying. I was terrified they'd figure out what was going on at home. I never thought about asking for help or telling them. I just wanted her to be okay and not be in pain or be sick. I never imagined that if I actually told someone in the medical field they might actually save us. Karen was in the medical field and she definitely did not save me as a child. I was relieved to be released from the hospital and be able to go home. I swore that would be the last time he ever hurt MY children. But it wasn't the last. It was only the beginning.

It was around this time, Brandon felt the need to go to college. He had the military GI bill which would pay for it, so we up and moved to Utah for him to attend BYU. He went ahead of the kids and me and found a house to rent. We packed up all our furniture and belongings and drove the U-Haul from Washington to Utah with two little babies in tow. He drove the moving truck with his vehicle towed behind, and I drove the children in my car. It was on this drive, this very long drive, I realized again, that I was moving away from family and friends to a place I knew no one. A place where like in California, I would be isolated and he would be stressed, which meant more anger outbursts.

As I followed that moving truck through mountain passes and through roads lined with big evergreen trees, I knew I wanted to escape. I couldn't continue on like this. I didn't want my children to continue on like this. I didn't see a way out unless we died. And if it wasn't by Brandon's hands then I would have to do something.

It was at that time, I can honestly say I became depressed to my core. I drove and daydreamed about driving the car off the road to our deaths. There would be no more pain, no more suffering. He couldn't hurt me or the children anymore. It would look like an accident. No one would be the wiser. But as I thought deeper and deeper about following thru with this action, I looked in the backseat seeing my smiling babies. They were content with me. They trusted me. How could I ever bring harm to them like driving off the road to our deaths? These were MY children. I would not give up. I would not. I couldn't. So I didn't.

We got settled into our new Utah residence. It was a huge brick rambler house with a daylight basement, with a large yard for gardening and beautiful amounts of green ivy crawling and enveloping the front entrance. It was a house which wanted to hide, much like I did so often in my life from those who were angry. The main floor had the kitchen with lots of sunlight, a living room, and three bedrooms and a bathroom. The daylight basement had a second living room with a fireplace, and two more bedrooms, a bathroom, and a large cellar pantry which kept nice and cool during the summer. The house was older and had dark wooden interior paneling and shag carpet throughout. But it was in a nice neighborhood, and the dogs (Raisin and Brandi) loved the large fenced yard.

We moved in early summer so he'd have enough time to get settled before classes began, and for me to find a job. I was unable to transfer my bank position, so I had to say goodbye to a managerial position which I had worked so hard to attain in the ATM processing department. I had worked hard and become the fastest 10-key processor. I was rewarded with managerial duties, to eventually being asked to write the step-by-step keystroke manual for the department for ATM processing. I later found out, this was used after I left to computerize everything and shut down the department.

The first job I was able to get was a tele-marketer for Mormon produced family video sales for the Mormon Church. I hated calling people and trying to sell things. Cold calling is not my gift. I lasted two weeks and then I had to leave. It just wasn't for me. Brandon had decided he was not going to work at all, and focus solely on school. It would be up to me to get a job that covered all the bills.

I started looking through the newspapers and noticed an ad looking for women to be escorts for businessmen for dinners and parties. The job would pay thousands! I had no idea what the duties of an "escort" were, but from the advertisement, it sounded easy! All I had to do was look pretty, dress up and be of good conversation at dinner parties. I could do that. So I called the agency's number. They seemed very polite and nice asking all about me. Then they asked me how tall I was, and when I told them I was only 5'1," they said I didn't qualify for the job, as they were looking for taller women.

I was so distraught and felt once again, not good enough; I was an ugly duckling. When Brandon came home from school that day, I told him about the ad and the conversation with the agency and their denial for my hire. He looked at the ad and began to laugh. He had to explain to me what an "escort" meant. I was so naïve, even at 25 years of age. I'm glad I didn't get hired. It was a good laugh, but it didn't change the ping of pain once again in not being wanted by others. Not being good enough, or the "ideal."

I finally landed a job at a family owned payroll processing company in the town next over from Orem where we lived, in American Fork. It was a friendly and close knit company of a few dozen employees. I was warmly welcomed, taught my duties and fit right in. My fast ten-key came in handy and I was proud of my work there. I was also proud of my work at home. I had the best garden I had ever had. I had apple boxes full of cucumbers and tomatoes which I would bring to the office because of the abundance. I had carrots and beans and peas. I canned so many jars of salsa and spaghetti sauce that fall, I felt like a proper Mormon wife. The sunshine was good for my soul too.

The heat reminded me of the Canadian prairies and the farm as a child. I was happy in my work and in my gardening. But I continued to be reminded of my failures as a wife by Brandon. Nothing I could do seemed to calm him or make him happy. Nothing. The extra stress of school was difficult and more than he had anticipated. While I worked and the kids went to a babysitter, he would attend classes and do his homework. The babysitter was a co-worker's daughter and was on my way to work every day.

One day, I received a phone call at work. The front desk said it was urgent and from my husband. As I sat at my desk and took a deep breath, I answered the phone. I could tell right away, Brandon was in one of his rages again. My daughter had been sick and so the kids didn't go to the babysitter that day. That weekend I had to take her into the doctor because she had a temperature of 103, had bright neon diarrhea and would just lay on the floor in a comatose state. I was so concerned. It turned out she had E. Coli and was severely dehydrated. She stayed a while in the hospital until she as better, but they encouraged her to stay home and rest for a few more days. Since Brandon didn't have class that day, he said he could do his homework and watch the kids. My daughter was 2 years old and my son was only 11 months old.

He yelled over the phone to me that I needed to get home and get home NOW!

"I'm done with these kids! You need to get your ass home NOW!" he screamed over the phone at me. He was beyond furious. I had no idea what he had done with the children.

"Where are the children?" I asked frantically.

"They're locked in the back bedroom where I don't have to deal with them anymore! Now get your ass home!"

My babies were locked in a room on their own! I told my office I needed to go home right away as there was an emergency at home. I couldn't explain, I just needed to get home.

I was so scared at what he had done to the children. Were they hurt? Were they alive? When I arrived home, I didn't see or hear them anywhere. He was sitting in the living room, enjoying a cold drink sitting in the lounge chair in his summer shorts watching the Simpsons. He was calm and relaxed. But there were no children anywhere. I asked him gently where the children were. He glared at me and then pointed towards the hallway and kept watching the TV.

I quickly went to the locked extra bedroom down the hallway and found the children in there. It was an extra bedroom with no furniture in there. We would sometimes use it as their playroom. In the far corner I saw my son, quietly sitting, huddled holding his blanket, tears in his eyes, but not a sound. My daughter was on her hands and knees scrubbing the shag carpet with a cloth, sobbing and crying to herself.

"I'm sorry. I'm sorry. I clean. I clean," over and over she cried and mumbled.

I stopped her and looked at what she was trying to clean up. It was feces. I paused and looked around the room. It was everywhere. On the walls and on the floor. Even on her brother.

"It's ok sweetie. You don't need to clean." She buried her wet face in my shoulder and bawled, still crying, "I'm sorry, I'm sorry, I clean, I clean."

After I calmed her, and cleaned the room, I got the kids fed and down for naptime. I went into the living room and stood in front of his Simpson show and asked what had happened. He finally looked at me and told me how they were interrupting his show so he locked them in the room. An hour later when he went to check on them there was shit everywhere. He got upset and told my daughter to clean up the mess and locked them back up. That's when he had called me at work.

I was dumbfounded and trembling by what I had seen. A child so scared hiding in a corner crying and mute. Another child so terrified she was repeating to herself an apology trying to scrub a carpet clean at the age of two. I didn't know what to do. This wasn't normal. This wasn't okay. I was beyond words. I was in shock at the trauma which I had allowed my children to experience that morning. I was afraid at what had happened to them to make them so scared in that room; Scared of him. What had he done to them? Why was she crying so profusely and scrubbing? What had he said and done to her? I made sure from then on, if the kids were sick, I would stay home. He was never going to babysit them himself again.

A few weeks later was my son's first birthday. I had made a chocolate cake and we were to have a small family celebration with just the four of us. Of course babies and cake always lead to a mess. I was prepared for it and joyous for this occasion, but Brandon didn't handle messes well. I had made spaghetti, which everyone loved, with the fresh sauce made from the garden. Soon things were getting messy, and Brandon was getting on edge. I promised to clean everything up; he didn't need to do anything.

We barely finished the birthday party, when he stormed off into the living room away from the mess in the kitchen and dining room to work on his homework and watch TV. I cleaned up the kids in the bath, and set them in the living room with their toys, while I cleaned up the kitchen and the dining room table. Soon Brandon was yelling at the kids, as they were interrupting "his TV time." I went into the living room to ask him to just watch them for a few more minutes while I finished up.

That was it; he blew his rage into full steam. He picked up the large heavy wooden coffee table and flung it on the floor where it shattered into pieces and shards. The brunt of the broken table landed just inches away from where my son was sitting on the floor. If it had hit him, he'd have killed him. It would have landed squarely on his head; his soft beautiful blonde little head.

The next day at work, while the kids were back safe at the babysitter, and Brandon was at school, I sat at my desk that Monday morning and realized something for the first time: If we don't leave, he's going to kill us.

CHAPTER ELEVEN

THE ESCAPE

It's a hard road to get to a point of "fight or flight" in a relationship. Sometimes it's a conscious choice, and sometimes things in our bodies just kick into gear and we encounter a strength we never thought we had, or too long ago had forgotten existed. I knew my number one responsibility was the safety of my children; it pounded in my very blood. How was I going to keep them safe?

My son could have died on his first birthday. The following weekend was our sixth wedding anniversary. I ended up with a bruised cheek. Nothing new there. As, so many times before, I applied the necessary cover-up and went to work the follow day. September of 1999 would turn out to be the defining moment of my life, and of our lives. I was called into the owner's office later that day. The door was closed behind me, and seated with the owner was some of my co-workers and manager. There was concern in the eyes.

"Pam, what happened?" My hand instantaneously rose to my face to cover, what I had already covered, my bruised cheek, while my words said "what do you mean?"

My very action of trying to hide, ultimately exposed my lie.

"Pam, this isn't the first time we've noticed. You just say the word, and we all are here to help." I was speechless. I could only sob and cry. No one had ever said they would help. That they could help. That they noticed and cared. That there was actual hope to end this. I burst open and shared everything to them. The long six years of torment.

"We can and will help you Pam." I spent the next month in a flurry of plans. It felt like I was living two lives; one with him, and the other building a new life.

Brandon's sister arrived the following week for a visit from Washington. He had asked her to bring his guns with her. I knew this, and it terrified me. When she arrived at the house, I was at work, the kids at the babysitters, and him at school. She called me all bubbly and joyous about her arrival, to let me know she had made it, and asked where to unpack the guns. I told her where the spare key to the house was, but asked her to go downstairs to one of the spare rooms before she unpacked the guns, and then call me back. She could hear in my voice the urgency of her adhering to this simple request.

"What the hell has been going on here??!!!" She called me back asking.

In a Mormon neighborhood where everyone likes to keep good appearances, one does not put out their TRUE garbage on the corner for pick up, especially a pile of broken furniture for everyone to see. So I had stored all of his broken rage items in one of the spare rooms downstairs. It was full. The coffee table was the latest addition to its broken stockpile. I finally shared the truth of the last six years with his sister. Everything. The hospital visits. The kids. Everything. At the end, his sister was silent over the phone.

"Please, whatever you do, don't unpack those guns," I pleaded. There was silence.

"I need to call my father. I'll call you back." About an hour later she called me back. She had told her father everything and he sternly told her to not unpack the guns. She was instructed to lie and say she accidentally forgot them. We were safe. For now.

Over the next month, I secretly cashed out my old employee stocks from the bank and set up a new bank account. The bank card came in the mail to the house. He got to the mailbox before I did that day. Shit! I feared that he had figured it all out. He knew I was trying to escape. When he confronted me about the new bank card that came in the mail when I got home from work that day, I lied.

"Oh, that. I have been given an expense account and that's the bank card for it," I responded so smoothly he didn't even question it. Thank God! I passed through the first hurdle.

I called and told Dad what was going on, and he secretly sent me money for an attorney.

"Don't tell Karen. This is between you and me. The safety of you and the children is most important and is priceless. You get the best lawyer. Period."

My workplace co-workers were now aware of the events and plans. They helped me find an apartment. They recommended an attorney. The wheels were rolling faster than I could handle. Every day I left the house to go to work, taking the kids to the babysitter, while he went to school, only to do meetings between work with apartment manager contract signing and lawyer meetings. When I was home and he wasn't, I began placing bright circular garage sale stickers on the underside of furniture, to mark which items we'd take with us. My co-workers had volunteered man-power and several pickup trucks. All I had to do was say the time and place and they'd be there. And so it was determined.

The day of the escape was Friday, October 1st. I took the children to the babysitters. She in turn was taking them away from her house as the lawyer had recommended. We did not want Brandon showing up at her place in anger with her there alone with the children. So off they went on an all-day field trip. After Brandon left for school, I went back to the house, and soon after rolled up several pickup trucks, men and women co-workers with boxes, and wrapping tape and tissue. I was shaking so terribly. I felt my knees were about to give out from under me. Was I really doing this? Could I really get away?

The ladies took charge and were organized, asking me what needed to get packed up. All the children's beds and rooms and items. Some basic dishes and pots. All children's pictures on the walls. The men began taking the basic furniture I would need and loading it up in their trucks, and strapping it down. In only one hour, we were packed up. Dressers, clothes, toys, beds. The basics. I had to leave the dogs though. My new place didn't allow animals. One of my co-workers asked if I wanted her to find a new home for them. I told her, I'm sure they will be fine.

We drove the few miles as a caravan to my new apartment. Everyone pitched in and got everything unpacked and set up. As everyone was leaving, the owner of the company, hugged me, held my hands, and squeezed a few hundred dollar bills into my hands. "For groceries and anything else you need to restart your life." And then he left.

I was alone in silence in our new place. I stood there in numbness. And then I collapsed to the floor. There were tears, but I didn't register if it was of joy or fear. It had been such a whirlwind of a morning. I took the afternoon organizing and grocery shopping. Then the babysitter brought the kids home to me directly that evening in the cover of dark. She was going to be out of town for the next few days, so that she wouldn't have to deal with Brandon. He was served the restraining order and separation papers when he arrived home later that afternoon from school.

From what I heard, he was pissed. He was hurt that he had been deceived. He went straight to the babysitters, the neighbor's said, pounding and kicking on her door. But no one was home. Next he broke down in the bishop's office crying with apologies. This was the same bishop who had told me to leave for our safety earlier in the month. Something Brandon didn't know I had done. I had two bishops and his own family tell me to leave. Finally his family had begun to tell me their own truths of his anger episodes. About holes in his family's home from his own anger over the years. Why hadn't they told me about this before?! I was furious at their silence all these years. I felt slightly betrayed that their silence had led to my continued silence, thinking they wouldn't believe me or understand. But alas, they understood far too well about his anger. They knew his anger first hand. That first night in our new home, my children slept with me. All of us in one bed together. Finally safe.

It was the weekend. We didn't need to go out of the apartment. We didn't need to go anywhere. The lawyer confirmed he had been served the restraining order, and that he was clearly aware he was not to go near the kids or me. He was not to show up at my work or the babysitters. I returned to work on Monday after the weekend. He called my office. I didn't take his call. Deep down I knew this was the end, but somehow I had told my lawyer not to file for a divorce, only separation. I thought maybe he could get counseling and we could be a family again.

By the end of the week I was served divorce papers by his lawyer. He was done. By the end of the next weekend, I got a phone call from his sister telling me that my dog, Brandi, was dead. Brandi had supposedly gotten out of the yard and had been killed in the street by a car. I thought they'd be safe if I left them with him. I know it wasn't a car that killed her.

October held a court hearing, where he showed up without his lawyer. The court would allow him supervised visitations with the children. It was to be at a court liaison facility. I would drop off the children, and then he would arrive afterwards so there would be no interaction between us. The visit was to be for an hour. I bundled up the children in their warm winter coats that scheduled evening of the visit and into the car seats in the mini-van and drove to the facility. I met the supervisor of the visit, Thomas, got the children settled in, and left. It was already dark outside and the winter chill of the Wasatch Mountain range was coming into the Orem valley below. I drove home, and sat in the silence. I hadn't even been gone thirty minutes when my phone rang. It was Thomas.

"Come back. The visit had to be terminated early. Come get the children."

"But I don't understand. Is everything alright?" I asked.

"I'll explain when you get here." Thomas said.

I could feel something wasn't right. The visit was supposed to be longer. What had happened? When I arrived, there were other staff spending time and sitting with the children. Thomas took me aside and explained what had happened.

The visit wasn't even ten minutes in, when Brandon touched the back of my daughter's neck, stroking her, when she reacted by crawling under a table, wrapping her arms tightly around her knees drawn up to her chest, begun rocking herself, and crying, "Owie Daddy."

Thomas terminated the visit at that point deeming it unsafe emotionally for the children. He told me her reaction was not normal, and was symptomatic of a child who's been abused, even groomed or worse. He said he would report this to the court, and reminded me that Brandon was not to see the children unsupervised under any reason. It was a court order, and if I chose to break that order, I could lose the children myself.

When I brought the children home from the visit that evening and got them in the front door of the apartment, I suddenly got a whiff of Brandon's cologne, as I closed the door. My heart raced in absolute terror. Had he figured out where we lived? Had he been in the apartment while I was gone? Why was his smell in our new home?

I left the children at the front door, and quickly searched our small apartment. I looked in closets and under beds. He wasn't here. So why was his smell? I went back to the children sitting on the front entryway still bundled in their winter coats. His smell was on them from the visit. I was ashamed of myself for my panic. But I wasn't going to have his smell in my house ever again. I gave the kids a thorough bath and washed their clothes. The song "I'm going to wash that man right out of my hair" has never come so close to being true.

For the next week, my daughter wouldn't sleep in her own bed. She would scream in the middle of the night "owie Daddy, owie!!" I didn't know what to do.

My lawyer informed me that the court wanted her to go through a physical exam for sexual abuse. I wanted to throw up. He wouldn't have. He couldn't have. Did he? I took her for the exam. They explained to me the procedure and how it was non-evasive. They would simply spread her legs, have a magnifying glass and bright light to see if there had been any damage. Her exam was inconclusive. She wouldn't let them do what they needed to do. The moment they went to spread her legs, she screamed and cried "owie Dady, owie!" They may not have gotten their legal proof but I had mine. The court cancelled all his supervised visits until further notice. He was to have no contact. No exceptions.

Christmas was coming, and November brought the financial reality of my situation. The min-van was repossessed because I couldn't't make payments and pay rent. I had to apply for food stamps and assistance. Brandon was not paying any child support. It was one thing when I was homeless or eating watered flour pancakes, but I could not have my babies live that way. I got into a therapy support group through the battered Women's Clinic.

My work was extremely supportive. The boss was always coming around to my desk checking in to see how we were doing. I kept my focus on work and on the children, the two joys in my life. The new Mormon Church ward I began attending was able to get me a beat up old car to get to and from work. Then one night the week of Christmas, the doorbell rang at our apartment. I answered it cautiously, as I had done since we left, always on edge that he had finally found us. What I found were bags and bags of groceries and wrapped presents. No one was around to thank. I knew it was either my work place or the church. I was in tears with the numerous trips back and forth to bring all these bundles of love and care inside. It would be a Christmas never to forget.

The months continued to move forward into the New Year. I ended up needing to get a new lawyer, as my first was dis-barred. I didn't ask why, but I got the best lawyer the next time around.

Rose was her name. She was an older woman in her mid-60's with brightly dyed rose-colored hair. She was a few inches taller than me, but she was a giant in the court room. She was respected and revered when she walked into that room. Everyone knew who she was. The final court appearance for the divorce was fairly quick and painless. I was terrified to appear, but Rose assured me I would be safe and everything was going to be okay. Brandon never showed up. I got sole custody of the children. He had no visitation rights. There was a four year protection order given. He had to pay child support. I was allowed to move out of state and back home to Washington. Done. The divorce was finalized. It was finally done. I moved back immediately to Washington the following month in May.

We were free. Truly free. At last. And another journey starting at mile zero began.

CHAPTER TWELVE

FAITH AND HEALING

I remember being about six years old and dusting the books on the shelves for Karen. They had to be done a certain way. You had to take out each book individually, dust all four sides, the spine and the pages, dust the spot in which it came from, and then set it back in its spot nice and squarely even with the other books. Then do the next book. And the next book following. There were dozens of shelves of books in our home. There were also nick-knacks on the shelves. Each item had to be perfectly dusted and re-set back in its exact place, otherwise I would be yelled at and told to redo them all over again. This task seemed to take hours.

There was one book I dreaded dusting. In fact, truth be told, I avoided it and dusted around it; never touching it. The Bible. Karen had told us how we were sinful children and how horribly behaved we were. And at age six, I already knew and comprehended that God was a mighty God who had anger just like Karen and would strike me down if I was impure in my thoughts and actions. I thought if I touched that Bible, lightening would surely strike me dead. I believed this to my core and it terrified me. So I didn't touch it and I dusted around it with my little fingers tucked tightly for protection in the dust rag cloth.

But I also learned about a God in Sunday School who loved all the little children. I learned that I could say the Lord's Prayer anytime I needed

God to be with me. And so began the Two-Gods of the world in my mind. There was Karen's God of wrath and judgment, and then there was my God who I could pray to in the dark of the night when she wasn't watching over me. My God was with me in the darkness of my bedroom, her God was judging me in the daylight hours while she watched. My God brought calm, peace and comfort. Hers brought only fear.

Prayer has always been close to my heart for this reason I think. As a scared child, I could always talk to my God. Now God didn't talk back, even in spite of my pleading sometimes. I pleaded for a sign to verify that He existed.

"Just let me see Uncle Brian one more time. Bring him back just for me to see him so I know you're real." But Uncle Brian never appeared in my bedroom as a ghost.

When I prayed to my God, I always felt a calm come over me. All my trembling and fears of the day's yelling and hurtful hands went away. This was the case throughout all my youth. God was always there for me in my prayers. I never prayed for good grades on a test or a boyfriend. I never prayed to not be the ugly duckling or to take me away from Karen's anger. I simply prayed for God to be with me. For God to never leave me. I prayed for peace. God's peace.

When I was struggling to get pregnant with my first child, I finally prayed to God and released it all over to Him. That very night that I released it over to God, I had a dream. But this was more than a dream. I awoke from it not knowing if I was still dreaming or awake because it was so real.

In my dream I stood in the middle of a grass field. My bare feet on the cool grass, my toes able to dig gently into the moist soil. About 10 feet out from me in every direction, I was surrounded by a white cloud. Even above me, and yet somehow there was the presence of a bright sunny day with a blue sky. This cloud was not cold, but exuded warmth and gentleness. There was a strong and solid voice which spoke from the cloud, and yet it didn't just speak audibly, as the very words penetrated into my chest and hung there for me to not only hear but also feel.

"Hearken."

"Hearken."

"Hearken." It said. Over and over and over.

At the end of my dream which lasted the whole night, I felt something in my hand in the dream. I looked down towards the bright green fresh grass, and in my hand was a child's hand holding mine. And then I awoke. I was out of breath when I awoke. I could still hear and feel that voice and those words.

I can still hear and feel those words and that voice somedays. It was the next week after this dream which I found out I was pregnant. And this child, this beautiful daughter of mine, had precious imaginary friends when she was older after we escaped.

"Mommy, don't close the door yet. God and the angel aren't in the car yet."

And it was this same girl, who as she got into elementary school would read the Psalms and then write pieces of them on post-it notes and place them around the house to cheer me up. Yes, she is precious to me. Oh, so very precious.

Prayer continues to be a part of my healing and a deep part of my faith today. Mother Teresa was interviewed by Dan Rather once and asked what she said to God when she prayed. She shared that she listened to God. When asked what God said in return, she said, "He doesn't say anything; He just listens." I think this is profound, and I have experienced the same. I wish we all could experience this: God's powerful listening.

In my healing from the years of abuse in my life, I have learned that the power of listening is profound and immeasurable. When we are supplied space to be fully heard, it is healing. When we are gifted the service to hear another, it is humbling. Being able to be fully present without distraction for another is a gift; a priceless gift.

When the children and I returned to Washington, I was encouraged to get my daughter into therapy. She was only three years old, but memories begin at age two and a half, I was told. Who knows what she remembered and what she carried deep in her. She needed a place that would listen to her. Overlake Hospital in Bellevue had a children's therapy department. Their motto: "Children are to be seen, heard, AND believed." That was a drop-mic moment for me. Don't we all need to be seen, heard and believed?

When I left Brandon and Utah, I left the Mormon Church. Although they are wonderful people and helped me immensely along my faith journey and saved my life, I knew years earlier that the theology was not one I could follow or fully believe. So I returned to the Lutheran faith. Here I found grace again. A place where we can come to the table as broken and messed up souls, not having to present ourselves as perfect, but simply as we are. It is in this transparency that we will be accepted, loved, fed, and sent back out into the world with a God who will never abandon us. For too many years I felt unwanted. But I know God wants me. Always.

One of my therapists asked me when I returned to Washington and I tried to reconcile my relationship with Karen to no avail, asked, "Why do you keep running into the brick wall?" It was then I realized I just needed to feel accepted. Every child wants to be loved, wanted, and accepted by their parenting figure. I wanted to hear "I'm sorry." I wanted to hear "You are enough." But those words would never be heard: never spoken from Karen. When she died years later, she still wouldn't let me come to her bedside in an effort to finally reconcile. So, I had to learn that sometimes, you have to forgive on your own.

Forgiveness is truly one sided. I don't need the other person aware of my forgiveness for them. Forgiveness is a ME thing. It's where I let go of any desire for retribution or getting even. The person I forgive can be dead or alive, but the forgiveness action is solely inside of me. Forgiveness is the change which happens within me, not within them. They may never change, but I can still choose to forgive them.

For some, like me, God helps me get there, as do therapists. It's hard work. Sometimes, it's daily work, even hourly work. Ongoing and continually. Making the choice to forgive. But forgiveness is NEVER about being forced to forget. The old saying, "forgive and forget" is bullshit! If we forget, then we never learn. We don't learn about our own faults and tendencies to repeat the same choices and mistakes. If we forget, we CANNOT reconcile with another.

Ultimately reconciliation is not about forgiving and forgetting and moving on like nothing has ever happened. Reconciliation takes forgiveness one step further and requires both parties. Reconciliation is about naming the harm, both parties agreeing that they want to do better, and committing to building a *new and different relationship*. It doesn't deny the old broken relationship. In fact it stays in the rearview mirror to remind us where we have been, where we have moved on from, and from where we can never and should never go back to. But it is truly behind us. Reconciliation is facing forward and committing to the new path we are on together.

Reconciliation requires both parties, but forgiveness only requires one; the one who is hurt. The hardest part about forgiveness is realizing sometimes we never get to hear the words "I'm sorry." But I still have the choice to forgive.

As I have moved forward in life, I have not let my past define me. I have been molded by it, and I get to make the choice on if I will stay in the past or live into the future of what will be. I choose moving forward.

I choose releasing the ugly hurt feelings. Releasing the anger and the desire to get back at those who have hurt me. I choose to speak my truth and be heard. I choose life and living it to its fullest. I know I can do this because God is always with me. Listening to me. Hearing me. Comforting me through every hard step and skipping alongside me with every joyous step. I am not alone. And for the first time in my life, I also know that I am enough as I am.

As I received counseling when I left the abuse in Utah, I was encouraged to take up hand quilting for the first time. Sewing had always been associated with Karen and perfection and her abuse. But now I was encouraged to take pieces of fabric and sew them together to make something useful and beautiful. It became a deliberate act of resilience and a reflection of my own life. My broken pieces could be put back together and made into something beautiful again. With every stitch I made, I sewed, healed, and sealed the past into something other than what it was prior. With every stitch, I had the power to create what I was going to become and what this quilt was going to become. From dozens of pieces of fabric became something whole again and something which became a symbol of love and hard work. From a heap of pieces, became something beautiful. From a mess became something which would give comfort and warmth to another. But I didn't do it alone. I couldn't have done it on my own. There were so many voices I had to battle from my past with every silent stitch I made. Each stitch boldly silenced the negative voices, and I began to only hear the encouraging and affirming voices around me and in me, remaking and remolding me into who I truly was meant to be.

I am a beautiful and wonderfully made creation by God. I don't have to be someone I'm not. I don't have to be perfect. I can be broken and healing AND still be loved and wanted. Because ultimately, I trust that I, and every single person who is and has been in pain like me, IS A BELOVED CHILD of GOD.

EPILOGUE

INTO THE LIGHT

John 8:32 "...the truth will make you free." Too often we live in the shadow of fear. We fear losing our jobs or fear if we will be able to pay the rent. We fear if our kids will grow up to be good responsible citizens. We fear judgment if we fail in a marriage. So when we live in the shadows, we hold back sharing our darkest truths; sharing our truths about our fears.

It is my hope that this book sheds light into a darkness which still pervades our society: Domestic Violence. Too many hide in the shadows, afraid to speak their truths. Both the victims and the perpetrators. Both have shadows which harm them. The victim's shadows are evident in the harm they receive either physically, mentally, or spiritually. The victim's shadows linger with every breath they take and every action they do, even long past removal from the harmful situation. The bones and bruises heal usually, but the dominating voices in our heads can be hard to tackle and overcome. For the perpetrators of domestic violence, they suffer too, but in a way we often overlook.

Many victims will give excuses for their abuser; they had a bad day, they didn't mean too, they don't know any better because of their upbringing. The truth is, the abuser knows what they are doing is wrong; they just don't know how to control it. So their dark shadow is not being able to control their fear and anger which explodes onto the ones they promise to love and protect.

We must start bringing these truths into the light. When we speak our truths, healing begins. Both parties have more strength than they realize inside of them to speak their truths. When one digs down deep, faces the shadows of fear and speaks the light of truth into that shadow, it doesn't seem as daunting anymore.

Tell your stories my friends! Once I was confronted by my boss and co-workers, my shadows which I so desperately tried to conceal (literally even!) were exposed. Once a small shimmer of light shone into my shadows, there was hope and there was a breath of relief. Once I began to speak my truth openly, I began to have more power over my shadows. Light conquers the shadows. Truth is the light.

Matthew 5:16 "...let your light shine..." If you speak your truth, you will be able to stand in the light of day and be able to share your light with others. We are all created to be in community with each other. When we shed a blind eye to the harm of another, we are not shinning our own light forward. We are each called to care for humanity, to help others speak their truths, to end the shadows which imprison so many and cause harm.

I am not a therapist, but merely someone who has traveled a journey which is unfortunately not unique, but rather too often not spoken about. I encourage those who are victims of Domestic Violence to know clearly and boldly: YOU ARE NOT ALONE! There is help for you, for your children. Please reach out to professionals, police, therapists, church, friends, family, neighbors, and co-workers. You do not have to try to leave on your own. In fact, to be successful in breaking the cycle of abuse, you *must* have a support system in place when escaping. In the following pages are the national hotlines and websites to assist in your departure of violence. A violence which you did not make, nor do you deserve.

And to those who abuse, there is help for you too. Look in the mirror and acknowledge your shadows and get the help you need. Seek a therapist and be gut-wrenchingly honest about your abuses and your own hurt which brought you to do such actions on the ones you love. Separate yourself from those you are harming so that YOU can truly heal and be made new again.

Every year I lead a four day backpacking trip for those who care to do the final steps in finding their inner strength and letting go of their shadows. These groups of individuals have battled all sorts of grief and loss. It truly is grief when you chose to move forward from something in your life and let go of the past and forgive. When we embark on our hike, we are dropped off; there is no going back to the car if we are tired. It's a one way trip: but you are never alone. We are in community together every step of the way, supporting and cheering each other on. Pausing and resting, encouraging and comforting as needed.

Once we get to the top of the mountain pass, we can look back and see how far we have come. It is there that hikers have cried, shouted, danced, or even cursed and shaken a fist at the skies above. But we also then make the choice to move forward over the pass, leaving behind our past steps, letting them go in the dust, never to retrace them again. Many on the uphill climb will say they can't do it and want to give up. But there is no going back, and no one is being left behind. We all move forward together in community. When we come back down the other side of the mountain, I commonly hear, "I didn't think I had it in me. I didn't know I had that inner strength."

Yes, my dear friends, you have it in you. You have it in you to make a choice and change your path. I'm not saying it's going to be easy, in fact, it's going to be the hardest thing you've ever done. But trust me, it's worth it. So speak your truth into the light, and be the light for others to get out of their shadows. You no longer need to be the victim, you can be the survivor!

RESOURCES FOR VICTIMS
AND SURVIVORS
OF DOMESTIC VIOLENCE

NATIONAL CRISIS ORGANIZATIONS AND ASSISTANCE:

The National Domestic Violence Hotline
1-800-799-7233 (SAFE)
www.ndvh.org

National Dating Abuse Helpline
1-866-331-9474
www.loveisrespect.org

National Child Abuse Hotline/Childhelp
1-800-4-A-CHILD (1-800-422-4453)
www.childhelp.org

National Sexual Assault Hotline
1-800-656-4673 (HOPE)
www.rainn.org

National Suicide Prevention Lifeline

1-800-273-8255 (TALK)

www.suicidepreventionlifeline.org

National Center for Victims of Crime

1-202-467-8700

www.victimsofcrime.org

National Human Trafficking Resource Center/Polaris Project

Call: 1-888-373-7888 | Text: HELP to BeFree (233733)

www.polarisproject.org

National Network for Immigrant and Refugee Rights

1-510-465-1984

www.nnirr.org

National Coalition for the Homeless

1-202-737-6444

www.nationalhomeless.org

National Resource Center on Domestic Violence

1-800-537-2238

www.nrcdv.org and www.vawnet.org

Futures Without Violence: The National Health Resource Center on Domestic Violence

1-888-792-2873

www.futureswithoutviolence.org

National Center on Domestic Violence, Trauma & Mental Health

1-312-726-7020 ext. 2011

www.nationalcenterdvtraumamh.org

National Runaway Safeline

1-800-RUNAWAY or 1-800-786-2929

www.1800runaway.org

CHILDREN

Childhelp USA/National Child Abuse Hotline
1-800-422-4453
www.childhelpusa.org

Children's Defense Fund
202-628-8787
www.childrensdefense.org

Child Welfare League of America
202-638-2952
www.cwla.org

National Council on Juvenile and Family Court Judges
Child Protection and Custody/Resource Center on Domestic Violence
1-800-527-3233
www.ncjfcj.org

Center for Judicial Excellence
info@centerforjudicialexcellence.org
www.centerforjudicialexcellence.org

TEENS

Love is respect
Hotline: 1-866-331-9474
www.loveisrespect.org

Break the Cycle
202-824-0707
www.breakthecycle.org

College Campus Safety Guide

DIFFERENTLY ABLED

Domestic Violence Initiative
(303) 839-5510/ (877) 839-5510
www.dviforwomen.org

Deaf Abused Women's Network (DAWN)
Email: Hotline@deafdawn.org
VP: 202-559-5366
www.deafdawn.org

WOMEN OF COLOR

Women of Color Network
1-800-537-2238
www.wocninc.org

INCITE! Women of Color Against Violence
incite.natl@gmail.com
www.incite-national.org

LATINA/LATINO

Casa de Esperanza
Linea de crisis 24-horas/24-hour crisis line
1-651-772-1611
www.casadeesperanza.org

National Latin@ Network for Healthy Families and Communities
1-651-646-5553
www.nationallatinonetwork.org

IMMIGRANT

The National Immigrant Women's Advocacy Project
(202) 274-4457
http://www.niwap.org/

INDIGENOUS WOMEN

National Indigenous Women's Resource Center
855-649-7299
www.niwrc.org

ASIAN/PACIFIC ISLANDER

Asian and Pacific Islander Institute on Domestic Violence
1-415-954-9988
www.apiidv.org

Committee Against Anti-Asian Violence (CAAAV)
1-212- 473-6485
www.caaav.org

Manavi
1-732-435-1414
www.manavi.org

AFRICAN-AMERICAN

The Black Church and Domestic Violence Institute
1-770-909-0715
www.bcdvi.org

LESBIAN, BI-SEXUAL, GAY, TRANSGENDER, GENDER NON-CONFORMING

The Audre Lorde Project
1-178-596-0342
www.alp.org

LAMBDA GLBT Community Services
1-206-350-4283
http://www.qrd.org/qrd/www/orgs/avproject/main.htm

National Gay and Lesbian Task Force
1-202-393-5177
www.ngltf.org

Northwest Network of Bisexual, Trans, Lesbian & Gay Survivors of Abuse
1-206-568-7777
www.nwnetwork.org

Trans Lifeline
877-565-8860
www.translifeline.org

ABUSE IN LATER LIFE

National Clearinghouse on Abuse in Later Life
1-608-255-0539
www.ncall.us

National Center for Elder Abuse
1-855-500-3537
www.aginginplace.org

MEN

National Organization for Men Against Sexism (NOMAS)
1-720-466-3882
www.nomas.org

A Call to Men
1-917-922-6738
www.acalltomen.org

Men Stopping Violence
1-866-717-9317
www.menstoppingviolence.org

LEGAL

Battered Women's Justice Project
1-800-903-0111
www.bwjp.org

Legal Momentum
1-212-925-6635
www.legalmomentum.org

Womenslaw.org
www.womenslaw.org

National Clearinghouse for the Defense of Battered Women
1-800-903-0111 x 3
www.ncdbw.org

Legal Network for Gender Equity

nwlc.org/join-the-legal-network/

Domestic Violence Legal Empowerment and Appeals Project
www.dvleap.org

ACKNOWLEDGEMENTS

There are so many people who have helped me on my journey, those I have briefly mentioned in my story, and the hundreds of others who are not.

First I'd like to thank my children for being the joy in life. It was because of you which didn't allow me to give up. My daughter for her 18th birthday wished for us to get our first tattoo together. She picked it out; part of the sentence would be on my foot and part on hers. Mine reads, "For them I'd risk it all" and on my daughter's "…because of her I shall not fall." Thank you my dear loves of my life!

I am so grateful for my new husband, where there is proof that real and healthy love can actually happen. For his patience and support and encouragement in my writing. For his loving arms which have held me during the rough moments of this writing as I re-lived and wrote my story. Thank you Jonathan for showing me unconditional love, grace, and support in all things.

I am grateful for those who helped me escape. For my co-workers in Utah, to family and friends who helped me when I returned to Washington. I am grateful for the justice system, my lawyer Rose, and for the care and wisdom and quick action by Thomas at the supervised visit center. You saved us. Literally. Thank you.

I am grateful beyond words to my mother Ann, who in spite of her heart-ache, never gave up hope that her children would return to her again someday, and who never gave up faith that God was holding her through all the pain. I am grateful for the years following my divorce which I was able to rebuild my lost relationship with her. For her love of her grandchildren and our visits to Canada. For her undying example of faith and prayer. Too soon did she die in 2015, but I am grateful for the years I was granted with her, to hear her truth and give light to her shadows.

I am grateful for my friends and professors who have encouraged the writing of this book. My only hope is that it will be an example for others; a place of inspiration and hope in getting out of any domestic violence situation. Thank you to my friends who have read and re-read my manuscript and gave editing guidance; Nancy Belvin, Brenda Ulinski, Donna Linn, Kim Kusilek, and Paul Ingram.

A very special thank you to my main editor, and the woman who began this journey of writing for me, Professor Annemarie Russell. It was in her creative writing class back in 2011, where she asked students to write the prologue to our memoir (if we were to ever have one). It was from this first writing, which still stands as this book's prologue, which she passionately encouraged me to finish telling my story. Thank you Annemarie for your confidence in me, my story, and my writing.

Everyone has a story to share. Everyone's story IS important enough to share. May we all have the courage to share it someday.